THE
BEER
BIBLE

Willie Simpson

PLUS THE BEER SOMMELIER'S HANDBOOK

Other book titles available from *The Sydney Morning Herald* and *The Age* stores:

Snap: Extraordinary Pictures by Award-Winning Photographers
Good Weekends Away, featuring 100 of the best short-break holidays
The SMH Good Food Guide, a guide to Sydney's best dining experiences
The Age Good Food Guide, a guide to Melbourne's best dining experiences
Gallipoli: Untold Stories, commemorating the campaign's 90th anniversary
The Big Picture, 175 years of articles and images from *The Sydney Morning Herald*
Reflections, celebrating *150 years of The Age*
Winter cookbook
Epicure Chocolate
Baby's Journey, a family record of those early years
Hundreds of Medical Myths and Misconceptions
Writing Good English: a concise guide to keeping it simple and getting it right
Best Letters to the Editor (Volumes 1 and 2)
The Best of Column 8 (Volumes 1 and 2)
Plus a range of *Word Puzzle*, *Sudoku* and *Crossword* titles

To find out more about these titles and other great offers please contact either
The SMH Store on 1300 656 059 or visit www.smh.com.au/store or
The Age Store on 1300 656 052 or visit www.theage.com.au/store

Copyright © 2006 John Fairfax Publications Pty Ltd.
201 Sussex Street, Sydney, NSW, 2000

The Sydney Morning Herald is the registered trade mark of John Fairfax Publications Pty Ltd.

The Age is the registered trade mark of The Age Company Ltd.

Publisher John Fairfax Publications Pty Ltd.
Author Willie Simpson
Chief sub Patrick Witton
Editorial assistant Bronwen Sewell
Cover design and internal page layouts Peter Schofield
Photography Mark Chew, Matt Strickland
Pre press The Age Imaging Centre.

Managing Editor, Fairfax Books Michael Johnston (02) 9282 2375
Senior Product Manager, Fairfax Enterprises Linda MacLennan (02) 9282 3054
Publishing Manager, Fairfax Enterprises Stephen Berry (03) 9601 2232
General Manager, Fairfax Enterprises Lauren Callister (02) 9282 3904
General Manager, Strategy and Enterprises Ben Way

Printed in Australia by BPA Print Group

ISBN 1 921190 22 1

THE
BEER
BIBLE

Willie Simpson

PLUS THE BEER SOMMELIER'S HANDBOOK

CONTENTS

INTRODUCTION

In the beginning was the wort (and the wort was unfermented beer) and the wort came from God. Or so our early ancestors must surely have thought when, miraculously, that wort turned into a brown, fizzy liquid that was delicious, nutritious and – best of all – mildly exhilarating.

These days, when beer is such a popular social beverage, it's hard to fathom that it was prized originally as a reliable food source. So prized, in fact, that it influenced civilisation as we know it, as man settled down from a nomadic existence as a hunter-gatherer and started raising crops and domesticating animals. Cereal crops were turned into beer and bread, and the rest – as they say – is history.

We can only hazard a guess at the circumstances that led to the first accidental brewing of beer – perhaps a quantity of grain stored in a ceramic pot was left out in the rain, got soaked, then warmed up under the sun until wild yeasts caused the liquid to froth and bubble. That first taste of beer must have seemed like a gift from the gods to some lucky drinker, especially when a wave of mild euphoria followed.

What we do know for certain is that barley, a wild grass, originated in the fertile delta of ancient Mesopotamia. There is evidence that – at least 6000 years ago – inhabitants in that area

were cultivating barley and brewing beer. Some anthropologists even believe that beer has been around in one form or another for more than 10,000 years.

Of course, that primitive beer would have been quite different from the modern version most of us enjoy, though it may have tasted a little like the winey, tart lambic beers from Belgium, which are still fermented with wild, airborne yeasts.

Hops are a relatively recent arrival in the long history of brewing, though various herbs and spices have been employed to bitter or season beer.

As for beer in Australia, John Boston is recorded as the colony's first brewer. He knocked up a batch of beer in the 1790s from malted maize and bittered it with the leaves and stalks of the cape gooseberry. It was a rough-and-ready beginning, improved upon a few years later by the successful hop grower James Squire. His legacy lives on, thanks to the Malt Shovel Brewery's range of craft beers bearing his name.

The sunbaked Australian climate wasn't kind to colonial brewers, who struggled to make English-style ales in often hostile conditions. Their plight is perhaps best summed up by the aptly named Hit and Miss Brewery that operated in the township of Hamilton, in southern Tasmania during 1850-1881. →

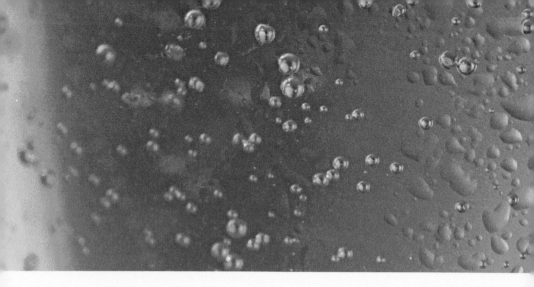

Things changed dramatically after the 1880s with the arrival of mechanised refrigeration, which enabled lager brewing to be conducted at controlled temperatures. An enterprising pair of brothers from New York – William and Ralph Foster – landed in Melbourne with the latest lager-making equipment and a German brewer; their Foster's Lager was launched in 1889 and took the local pub trade by storm.

This clean-tasting, chilled lager beer was a revelation to local drinkers and the "new" brewing methods soon eclipsed the old style of ale-making (although darker "old" ales are still brewed, including those made by Coopers in Adelaide).

It was also in 1889 that the number of breweries in Australia peaked at 307. It declined rapidly thereafter: the 20th century was volatile for the brewing industry, a time of closures, mergers and takeovers. By 1980, only 20 individual players remained. Their number shrunk further in the 1980s as more takeovers ensued, but the decline was offset by a new phenomenon – the rise of independent boutique or craft breweries.

In the past five years the number of craft breweries has doubled to 70-plus, with a new operator firing up virtually every month. The larger, established breweries, once suspicious of these brazen newcomers, have lately embraced the rising tide of

premium and craft beers. As a result, the Australian beer drinker
has never enjoyed so much choice.

It's funny how sometimes a single incident can capture
the spirit of the time. For me, it happened one sunny Sunday
afternoon at a lavender farm festival on the outskirts of
Melbourne. I was tracking down Beth Williams, co-owner of
Hargreaves Hill Brewing Company (with her husband and brewer
Simon Walkenhorst) – one of the smallest craft breweries in the
country. I eventually located her behind a stall, handing out beer
samples and bouncing a toddler on her hip while selling a six-pack
of porter to a silver-haired gent in a baseball cap. The gentleman
just happened to be Peter Manders, master brewer for our largest
beer-maker, Foster's. "It's good beer," he reported.

A couple of months later I interviewed Manders as he
celebrated 50 years with Carlton & United Breweries/Foster's.
What did the future of the Australia beer industry hold? "We're
going to see more and more newer products, which is exciting."

I'll drink to that.

Willie Simpson

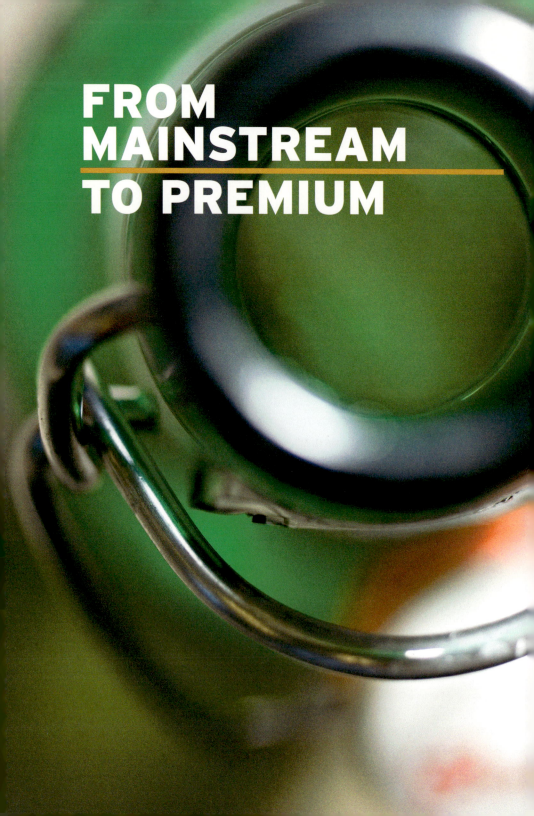

FROM
MAINSTREAM
TO PREMIUM

It's official — **Australians are** drinking less beer but, progressively, it's better quality. While the consumption of beer per capita has declined marginally over the past decade or so, the so-called "premium" segment continues to grow at a healthy rate of about 15 per cent a year.

Put those two factors into context and we get a clear picture of the average Aussie beer drinker spending less on mainstream brands and more on premium beers. It is part of a worldwide trend of consumers "stepping up" or "up-scaling" — to toss in a couple of marketing buzzwords — in terms of quality across all food and beverages, not just beer.

Recently retired craft brewery owner (and third-generation publican) Geoff Scharer recalls his father's Sydney pub in the 1960s having 12 different beer taps, all serving a single brand: Reschs Draught. Remember, this was the dark old days of the "six o'clock swill", when beer culture was all about bulk consumption and minimum choice for the consumer.

These days, walk into a city bar and you'll be be confronted with a choice of 12 different beers on tap, with a significant number of premium brands among them. It's now the consumer who drives the beer market, demanding more choice and more flavoursome beers. The boozy, blokey culture surrounding the amber nectar is fading fast, with more women enjoying premium beers than ever before.

PREMIUM-ISATION

The increasing *premium-isation* of the local beer market is being enthusiastically embraced by small and large brewers alike, but it begs the question: what exactly is a *premium* beer?

One dictionary describes *premium* as: "a sum above the nominal value of a thing; highly regarded; special; of highest quality." Therefore, a premium beer should represent a combination of higher price and, hopefully, higher quality.

"It comes down to the quality in taste, profiling and packaging," says Lion Nathan's spokeswoman Amy Lawrence. "Obviously, price comes into it as well."

"A premium beer is a special batch, looked after very well by brewers," says Dermot O'Donnell, Foster's beverage ambassador. "Part of the premium experience is the packaging – which connotes quality," he says. Crown Lager is the epitome of such a premium definition and it sells more than four million cases a year.

PREMIUM CATEGORIES

Within the premium segment, Lawrence identifies three separate categories: **domestic premiums** (Crown Lager, James Boag Premium, Cascade Premium, Hahn Premium, Coopers Sparkling Ale and the like), **international premiums** (Stella Artois, Guinness, Beck's, Heineken) and **craft beers** (James Squire, Matilda Bay, Little Creatures and a whole raft of "boutique" beers).

While the growth spurt in domestic premium beer has pretty well "matured", according to Lawrence, international premiums are "growing fastest" and the craft segment has unlimited potential.

Significantly, Lion Nathan has started producing leading imported brands Heineken and Beck's for the local market, while rival Foster's brews Guinness, Kilkenny and Stella Artois under licence. Other international premiums brewed in Australia or New Zealand include Carlsberg, Tuborg and Kingfisher. Such licensing arrangements presumably improve margins on these brands and make them more competitive with established domestic premiums (especially on tap).

Both our major brewers have invested heavily in the future of craft beers – Foster's owns Matilda Bay Brewing, while Lion Nathan controls the Malt Shovel Brewery and has a significant stake in Little Creatures Brewing.

But perhaps the most interesting domestic premium development in recent years has been the creation of Victoria Bitter Original Ale – effectively, a premium brand spin-off from a mainstream label.

THE VB PHENOMENON

So-called mainstream brands still account for about 90 per cent of the beer market, but there is no doubt that our beer-drinking habits have become more sophisticated and diversified. In the past, consumers chose a single brand for life, displaying one-eyed loyalty reminiscent of diehard footy fans.

Traditionally, beer drinkers opted for one of their local state brands, but things got a bit confused during the 1980s, when a hectic time of brewery takeovers and mergers meant state-based loyalty no longer made much sense. Carlton & United Breweries moved into NSW (acquiring the Tooth's Brewery) and, at one stage, Alan Bond owned breweries in three states. Further down the track, CUB bought out Power's Brewing in Queensland, and trans-Tasman Lion Nathan (half-owned by Japanese brewer Kirin) took over Bond Brewing and added South Australian Brewing to its portfolio.

By the late 1980s Victoria Bitter had become something of a de facto national brand. No one can explain the phenomenon in marketing terms, but when VB sales peaked one in every four beers drunk sported the famous red-and-green label. Ironically, while CUB was throwing bucketloads of advertising dollars at its other brand, Foster's Lager, it was VB sales that headed into the stratosphere.

Local beer drinkers can be a fickle lot, as evidenced by the fact that Foster's Lager accounts for less than one per cent of the beer market, despite being one of the top six beer brands on the international stage.

But the VB juggernaut has run out of puff lately, which makes the arrival of VB Original Ale all the more fascinating. This is a full malt ale with some genuine flavour, packaged with a retro label and priced well above the mainstream VB product. But who is it aimed at? When first launched, it sold for up to $6 a bottle across the bar and seemed designed to appeal to VB drinkers who wanted to stay loyal while trying something a little different.

Whatever the marketers were hoping for with VB Original Ale, it struck a chord with a wide range of consumers. Packaged in an unusual 18-stubbie carton, the beer was soon selling its socks off at bottleshops.

FROM MAINSTREAM TO PREMIUM

What impact it has on the core VB brand remains to be seen, but it looks like VB Original Ale has been created for a new breed of beer consumer: the repertoire drinker.

REPERTOIRE DRINKERS

"People drink different beers for different occasions," Amy Lawrence says, and the emergence of what she calls the "repertoire drinker" is very much the face of modern beer consumption. Rather than slavishly sticking to a single label, many drinkers tip-toe their way around a range of brands, depending on the situation – perhaps a mainstream beer for everyday drinking at home, a premium lager in the pub with workmates, a local craft beer to take to dinner and an imported brand when they're trying to impress.

Beer marketers are very interested in the reasons consumers choose certain brands, though often it's simply a spur-of-the-moment decision. Buying beer for home consumption is usually driven by price or what might be called "lifestyle" choice (an acquaintance of mine buys a low-carbohydrate brand because he reckons it helps his waistline).

In other situations, the choice of beer brand is a "badge" of sorts, according to those marketing types, where the drinker sees the brand as an extension of their social image or aspirations. Of course, none of this is an exact science and in many cases the beer marketers are trying to play catch-up on consumer trends; most of them are trying to anticipate the "next big trend".

What is very clear is that the beer consumer is driving the market, and this leads to all sorts of new brands and specialised beers being produced. Some disappear without trace in a matter of months, others find a gap in the market and become viable brands.

SEASONAL, SUPER OR SUB

The rise of seasonal or limited-edition beers is another recent trend, which also provides producers with a chance to test new beers on the market. Foster's used the Hobart-based Cascade Brewery in this way with its annual First Harvest Ale and the short-lived Four Seasons range of seasonal brews (some of which have evolved into regular, year-round brands).

In the latest beer marketing-speak, Cascade First Harvest Ale is a "super premium" brand which sells for about $17 a four-pack. Other brewers have launched brands in the "sub premium" category, which means they are priced slightly above the mainstream, but at less than premium levels (Boag's St George and Toohey's Extra Dry are examples).

Sometimes a brewery will release a limited-edition brand, seemingly without any expectation of making a profit – Boag's Leatherwood Honey Porter and James Squire Australian Strong Ale are two that come to mind: they were undoubtedly expensive to produce, but were sold at the same price level as their regular premium brands.

BOAG'S & COOPERS

Though still a long way behind the Big Two (Foster's and Lion Nathan) in terms of volume, J. Boag & Son and Coopers Brewery have both benefited immensely from the premium-isation of the local beer market. The Launceston-based Boag's Brewery "exports" the bulk of its production to mainland Australia, with its flagship premium lager selling more than a million cases a year, and the brewery is in the midst of a major expansion.

Coopers used to be regarded as a quaint, family-run brewery specialising in cloudy bottled ales. Since November 2001 it has operated from one of the country's most modern brewing plants and sales of its Pale Ale and Sparkling Ale keep breaking records. The company is still family-owned, after seeing off a recent aggressive takeover bid from Lion Nathan.

Meanwhile, the craft brewing industry continues to mushroom as more and more new players clamber aboard the bandwagon. Premium beers are here to stay.

GOLD, AMBER AND BLACK
(a guide to Australian beer styles)

The extended family of beer styles can be divided into ales and lagers. The division does get a little blurry at times, and succinct, non-technical definitions of these two main branches can present quite a challenge, but here goes.

Ales and lagers are generally brewed with different yeast strains, but the crucial distinction relates to fermentation temperatures. Ales are fermented at a higher temperature that encourages the development of fruity characters (or esters) and results in a full-flavoured, fruitier beer. Lagers are fermented at cooler temperatures and sometimes matured (or "lagered") for extended periods at even colder levels. This results in a beer that is crisper, less fruity, and designed to be drunk well-chilled.

In Australia, as we already know, the brewing industry largely switched from ale brewing to lagers after the arrival of refrigeration in the late 1800s. Unfortunately, most breweries simply maintained the same brand names, so we have a mish-mash of inappropriately named beers. Cascade Pale Ale, XXXX Bitter Ale, Victoria Bitter and Melbourne Bitter are examples of beer brands that started life as ales, but morphed into lagers.

GOLD, AMBER & BLACK

AMBER ALE

These malt-driven ales are based on a hefty dose of crystal malt, which produces a nice mid-palate complexity with caramel/toffee and sweetish Horlicks-like notes, and a moderate afterbitterness. James Squire Amber Ale found a ready market among lager lovers looking for more flavour without over-the-top bitterness.

Examples James Squire Amber Ale, Cascade Amber Ale, Little Creatures Rogers', Paddy's Amber Ale, Mildura Mallee Bull, Red Duck Amber Ale

AUSTRALIAN LAGER

This is a pale, golden lager, relatively highly carbonated, with moderate body and bitterness, to be served as cold as possible. That's my definition for the typical mainstream Aussie lager, which accounts for the vast majority of beer poured down throats in this country.

The defining characteristic of such beers is the inclusion of cane sugar, which results in the relatively lighter body. In countries like Japan and the US, rice and maize are used to similar effect, while European lagers are generally much fuller bodied, with 100 per cent malted barley employed.

These are usually more highly bittered, but this is balanced in flavour by the higher maltiness. In Australia, moderate body and bitterness go hand in hand.

Examples Victoria Bitter, Toohey's New, XXXX, Carlton Draught, Emu Bitter, Boag's Draught

BITTER

This term is widely misused in Australia. A true bitter is a version of an English-style pale ale served on tap — ideally by traditional hand-pump.

Examples Matilda Bay Stickler's Best Bitter, Lord Nelson Victory Bitter, Braidwood Best Bitter, Bulldog Best Bitter, Wig & Pen Pale Ale, Port Dock Black Diamond Bitter

BOCK

Bocks are strong lagers that can range in colour from pale gold to black, and shouldn't show any pronounced bitterness. In Germany, by law, a bock must have an alcohol content of 6 per cent, while a doppelbock (double bock) has to be 6.8 per cent. These are beers designed for sipping in the cooler months, rather than for quenching a thirst.

Examples Burragorang Bock, Hunter Bock, Redoak Bock, Sail & Anchor Brewer's Bock

BROWN ALE

Newcastle Brown Ale is the classic imported example of this English style – amber-brown in colour, malt-accented with a sweetish aftertaste and little discernible bitterness. This style is probably the inspiration for Kent Old Brown (formerly Tooth's Old), which is becoming harder to find.

Examples Kent Old Brown, Jamieson Brown Ale

DARK ALE

This style of beer employs plenty of dark-coloured malts (including black and roasted barley) to obtain their dusky hue and roasty flavour notes. Some have distinctive ale fruitiness, while others are cleaner and smoother, almost lager-like in palate.

Examples Toohey's Old, Coopers Dark Ale, Bulli Black, Robinson Dark Ale

DARK LAGER

Most German breweries produce a dark lager, which is labelled schwarzbier (black beer); such beers are coloured and flavoured with dark, higher-kilned malted barley such as chocolate malt and roast (or black) malt. The resulting palate has flavour notes of burnt toast, dark chocolate and coffee, without the heaviness of a stout or the strength of a dark bock. (Technically, it could be argued that both Toohey's Old and James Squire Porter fit into this category.)

Examples Matilda Bay Dogbolter, Macquarie Schwartzbier

GOLDEN ALES

Otherwise known as summer ales, this broad category includes beers that are designed as easy-drinking ales (generally aimed at mainstream lager drinkers). Many are brewed with a portion of malted wheat for a crisp, refreshing edge and feature hop flavour rather than substantial hop bitterness.

Examples James Squire Golden Ale, Cascade Blonde, St Peters Blonde (bottled as Green Star), Lord Nelson Quayle Ale, Red Hill Golden Ale, Paddy's Summer Ale

INDIA PALE ALE

This strong, highly hopped version of pale ale was developed in England during the 19th century for shipping to India, where the ready market included British troops and other expats. The classic IPA should feature plenty of hops, both in flavour and in a robust, lingering afterbitterness.

Examples James Squire IPA, Sail & Anchor IPA

IRISH RED ALE

The Irish drink more stout (mostly Guinness, of course) than any other nationality, and when they're not drinking the black nectar they are probably necking some red ale. Caffrey's, Kilkenny and Beamish Red are a few of the better-known brands, but there is a plethora of local brands as well, most with a big, malty mid-palate with lots of tannin and toffee notes, but a restrained bitterness.

Examples St Arnou Kildara, Ballyragget Irish Red Ale, Rust

PALE ALE (ENGLISH STYLE)

Classic English pale ales are often copper or amber in colour and were so named when they first appeared in the 19th century because they were considerably paler than standard ales. In Australia, the use of the name can be confusing, but it generally describes a well-bittered ale brewed with a portion of crystal malt.

Examples Coopers Pale Ale, Holgate Old Pale Ale, Mountain Goat Hightail Ale, Lord Nelson Trafalgar Pale Ale, Redoak Organic Pale Ale, Grand Ridge Gippsland Gold

PALE ALE (US STYLE)

This robust style of ale has taken the craft brewing world by storm, first in the US and, more recently, on these shores thanks largely to Little Creatures flagship brand. US-style pale ales are usually higher in alcohol, but are really defined by a huge burst of hop aroma, flavour and bitterness, using American-grown varieties such as Cascade and Centennial (with their telltale grapefruit and citrussy notes).

Examples Little Creatures Pale Ale, Matilda Bay Alpha Ale, Wig & Pen Brewer's IPA, MooBrew Pale Ale, Parkyn's Shark Oil

PILSENER

The city of Pilsen in Bohemia became the toast of Europe for the new style of golden lager it created in the 1840s, and most of the beer world has been trying to imitate it ever since. An authentic pilsener should be made exclusively with malted barley and European hops (including the Czech saaz variety), and lagered at cool temperatures for several weeks. Ideally, there should be some floral, aromatic hop character and a rich, malty palate balanced by substantial bitterness. Whether it's spelt pils, pilsner, pilzner or pilsener, this classic style is both the pinnacle of lager and the most misused descriptor.

Examples James Squire Original Pilsener, Matilda Bay Bohemian Pilsner, Little Creatures Pilsner, Bluetongue Pilsener, MooBrew Pilsner

PORTER

In the late 19th century porter was the most popular drink in London, but in more recent times the style has been eclipsed by its big brother – stout – and has all but died out. The original London porters were matured in huge wooden vats that undoubtedly would have contributed a lactic flavour note, absent from modern interpretations. Porters can be generally defined as a more easy-drinking version of stout.

Examples James Squire Porter, Porter Kembla, Nelson's Blood, Old Swan Brewery Porter, Hargreaves Hill Porter, Holgate Winter Ale

PREMIUM LAGER

Ideally, a premium lager should display a higher malted barley content and a more pronounced hop presence (often with the use of a European variety). It may be a relatively recent brand category, but Crown Lager has long been the local trendsetter in this field. Slick packaging defines the premium lager as something superior to the mainstream variety. No wonder green bottles abound and Heineken is unashamedly the inspiration for many of these beers.

Examples Cascade Premium Lager, Crown Lager, James Boag Premium Lager, Hahn Premium, Bluetongue Premium Lager, Gage Roads Pure Malt Lager

SCOTCH ALE

Not to be confused with malt-driven Scottish ale, Scotch Ale is a higher-alcohol style, usually amber in colour (due to the use of crystal and other coloured malts). This category has developed a cult following with local craft brewers in recent times.

Examples Redoak Wee Heavy, Red Hill Scotch Ale, Golden Dragon Celtic Ale

SPARKLING ALE

This style of bottle-conditioned ale was evidently popular in colonial times, when it generally meant a British-style ale with a lively ("sparkling") carbonation. The arrival of lager brewing meant it was a dying breed, although Coopers iconic cloudy ale survives, and there have been some flattering imitators in recent years. Coopers Sparkling Ale has a distinctive apricot-like fruitiness and a dry, yeasty finish.

Examples Coopers Sparkling Ale

GOLD, AMBER & BLACK

STOUT

Robust or stout porters — to give them their correct name — have outlived other members of the porter family, largely thanks to Arthur Guinness and his renowned Irish dry stout. In fact, stouts can come in all manner of styles — dry, medium, sweet (or milk), even oyster-laced versions. For some reasons never properly explained, most Australian mainstream breweries produce an admirable stout.

Examples Coopers Extra Stout, Southwark Old Stout, Cascade Stout, Carbine Stout, Sheaf Stout, Black Bart Milk Stout

STRONG ALE

This is a fairly broad category and encompasses high-alcohol ales that also have a pronounced hop flavour and bitterness. Colours can range from golden-amber through to dark brown, almost black; all might be referred to as "winter warmers".

Examples James Squire Australian Strong Ale, Grand Ridge Supershine, Grand Ridge Moonshine, Coopers Vintage Ale, Old Admiral, Old Preacher

VIENNA (OR RED) LAGER

As the name suggests, this style of beer evolved in Vienna during the 19th century and features slightly toasted, reddish malted barley now widely known as Vienna malt. This style of malt-accented lager displays delicate kilned malt characters with only a moderate level of bitterness.

Examples Matilda Bay Rooftop Red Lager, Hahn Vienna Red, Redoak Vienna Lager

WHEAT BEERS

European wheat beers (including hefeweizen, kristallweizen and wit) belong to the ale family and are fermented with specialised yeasts to produce distinctive flavour notes, such as clove, banana and bubble-gum. They are generally made from roughly equal proportions of malted barley and malted wheat. In the case of Belgian wit (or white) beers, unmalted wheat and oats are sometimes employed, while spices and dried orange peel are often used as additional flavourings. There should be a clear distinction between authentic European wheat beers and more standard beers that merely use wheat as an ingredient.

Examples Redback, Sou'west Wheat, Amber Hefeweizen, St Cloud, Burdekin Gold, Feral Belgian White

AND FINALLY ...

Some beers defy categorising and are conveniently lumped together in a separate section at beer awards. These include beers made with herbs, spices and fruit or various specialist styles including Belgian lambic, abbey and Trappist brews. Belgian lambic beers are fermented with feral, airborne yeasts and represent a link with a medieval form of brewing. Some lambics are infused with fruit.

Examples Jamieson Raspberry Ale, Holgate Double Trouble, Redoak Framboise Froment, Redoak Blackberry Hefeweizen, Redoak Belgium Choc-Cherry Stout, Beesting

CRAFTY
LOCALS

The Australian craft brewing industry is booming. New operations open at a rate of about one a month and, inevitably, others close down — so keeping track is a tricky business. Every effort has been made to compile the most up-to-date listing, including new businesses that are due to start brewing. Things change quickly, so check the brewers' websites for latest developments.

CONTRACT BREWING

As well as more than 70 operating craft breweries, there are all manner of independent beer marketers who don't actually own any beer-making equipment: their brands are produced under contract by someone else. St Arnou is undoubtedly the largest of such operations; others include a pair of gluten-free beers — Silly Yak (www.sillyyak.com.au) and O'Brien Gluten Free Beer (www.gfbeer.com.au). There are also Pike's Oakbank Beer (www.pikeswines.com.au), Bondi Blonde (www.bondibeer.com. au), Red Emperor Amber Ale and Leatherjacket Lager (both www. fishrockbrewery.com.au), Pigs Fly Pale Ale (www.pigsfly.net.au), Lucky Beer (packaged in a green Buddha-shaped bottle; www.luckydrinkco. com), Black Wattle Superior, Outback Export Premium Lager (www. baronbrewing.com), Crackenback Pale Ale and Bullocks Pilsner (www. snowymountainsbrewery.com.au), Piss and Piss Weak (www.pi55.com) and Dog House Wheat Beer (www.neaglesrock.com). Brewtopia has taken the concept of contract brewing a step further and offers custom-labelled beers that you can order and design on line (www.brewtopia.com.au).

AUSTRALIAN CAPITAL TERRITORY

Wig & Pen Brewery/Tavern

Canberra House Arcade, Civic, ACT 2601

Tel (02) 6248 0171

Website www.wigandpen.com.au

Brewer Richard Watkins

Wig & Pen brewer Richard Watkins recently clocked up 10 years service, a rarity in craft beer circles, with this Canberra brew-pub (which fired up in 1993). In that time he's brewed all manner of global beer styles (plus a few highly original ones), with countless seasonal numbers pumped out of the 500-litre microbrewery, as well as the established house brews. Real ale diehards love the handpumped ales (Wig & Pen Pale Ale, Bulldog Best Bitter, Brewers IPA), but the hoppy Pilsner, citrussy Kölsch, and luscious cream stout enjoy a strong following. On a recent visit, there were four distinctive wheat beers on tap, with the regular Belgian Blonde and Amber Hefeweizen complemented by a raspberry wheat ale and a decidedly tart Berliner Weiss. A haven of characterful beer in the nation's capital.

Beer selection Kiandra Gold Pilsner, Kamberra Kölsch, Ballyragget Irish Red Ale, Wig & Pen Pale Ale, Bulldog Best Bitter, Brewers IPA, Velvet Cream Stout, Amber Hefeweizen, Belgian Blonde

 ## NEW SOUTH WALES

Australian Independent Brewers

43 Topham Road, Smeaton Grange, NSW 2567

Tel 1300 724 978

Website www.a-i-b.com.au

Head brewer Brian Watson

Contract brewing has emerged recently as a significant part of the craft beer market. Lots of people, it seems, want to launch their own beer brands without the financial commitment of owning a microbrewery or automatic packaging equipment. (Indeed, most microbreweries produce keg-only beer or bottle by hand, and some are now contract brewing/bottling to reach wider markets). AIB principal Damian Silk saw a niche for an operation focused solely on contract brewing, and invested in a substantial freehold site in western Sydney, complete with the latest 6000-litre microbrewery, pasteurising equipment and high-speed bottling line. Head brewer Brian Watson was previously a director of St Arnou, which was foremost among AIB's first clients, along with online beer marketers Brewtopia (producers of Blowfly and customised labels for anyone who wants one). Other clients include Feral Brewing, Pike's Oakbank Beer and Silly Yaks.

Bluetongue Brewery

42 Stenhouse Drive, Cameron Park,
Newcastle, NSW 2209
Tel (02) 4955 4411
Website www.bluetonguebrewery.com.au
Head brewer Bruce Peachey

Launched in early 2004, Bluetongue Brewery tapped into the local Newcastle and Hunter Valley markets, using Tyrrell's Wines as a distributor. Bruce Tyrrell was an original shareholder, along with representatives from the Hunter Resort and the Queen's Wharf pub; Sydney ad man John Singleton has since invested heavily in the enterprise. Head brewer Bruce Peachey previously worked at Toohey's in a senior role. The flagship Bluetongue Premium Lager is moderately bittered, while Bluetongue Pilsener is highly aromatic and features the distinctive amarillo hop variety. Bluetongue's alcoholic ginger beer evolved from a house brew previously produced on-site at the Queen's Wharf Brewery.
Beer selection Bluetongue Premium Lager, Pilsener, Ginger Beer

Braidwood Traditional Ales

91 Wallace Street, Braidwood, NSW 2622
(02) 4842 1317
Contact braidwoodale@bigpond.com
Brewer Scott Watkins-Sully

This is a tiny, one-man brewing operation in the historic town of Braidwood in the southern tablelands of NSW. Scott Watkins-Sully is dedicated to producing English "real ale" and, after initially launching a range of bottled beers in 2004, he has since concentrated on a single, cask-conditioned ale which is served under hand-pump. His Braidwood ESB is available at a handful of Sydney outlets.
Beer selection Braidwood ESB

CRAFTY LOCALS

De Bortoli Brewery

De Bortoli Road, Bilbul, NSW 2680

Tel (02) 6966 0100

Website www.debortoli.com.au

Brewery manager Neal Cameron

Having owned a microbrewery for a decade, one of the country's best-known wine families is to launch a range of craft beers in November 2006. The 5000-litre brewing plant originally made beer for the Sovereign Brewery, Ballarat, in the late 1880s and has been re-housed at De Bortoli Wines HQ outside Griffith. Some keg beer will made for the local pub trade but production will be concentrated on bottled beers, with a pilsener, pale ale and bitter ale on the drawing board.

Five Islands Brewery

Corner Crown and Harbour streets,
Wollongong, NSW 2500

Tel (02) 4220 2854

Website www.fiveislandsbrewery.com

Brewer Tim Thomas

This bustling brew-pub, close to Wollongong's main sports stadium, entertainment centre and beachfront, is run by former local rugby league player Michael Bolt. The bar, in fact, overlooks the five small islands from which it takes its name, with beers named after local areas and identities. Regular beers include a flavoursome dark ale (Bulli Black), a delicately smoked porter (Porter Kembla), pleasantly bittered pilsener (Pig Dog Pilsner), an easy-drinking wheat beer (Longboard) and a robustly bittered IPA (the catchingly named Parkyns Shark Oil). As we go to press, there are plans to bottle the Longboard and Pig Dog Pilsner for the local Illawarra market.

Beer selection Dapto Draught, Pig Dog Pilsner, Parkyns Shark Oil, Longboard, Rust, Bulli Black, Porter Kembla

Hopping Mad Brewery

52/22 Scott Place, Orange, NSW 2800

Tel (02) 6361 0953

Website www.hoppingmadbrewery.com.au

Brewer James Peebles

This craft brewery in Orange has been operating since 2004. Its beers are available around the Orange region and in several Sydney outlets (check website for nearest).

Beer selection Hopping Mad Ale, Wheat Beer, Stout

Ironbark Brewery

52 Barnes Street, Tamworth, NSW 2340

Tel (02) 6762 2622

Website www.sssbbq.com.au

The Tamworth-based microbrewery makes beer for the chain of eight SSS BBQ Barns in NSW and Queensland.

Beer selection Ironbark Tawny Ale, Jesse James Ale

James Squire Brewhouse

22 The Promenade, King Street Wharf, Sydney, NSW 2000

Tel (02) 8270 7999

Website www.malt-shovel.com.au

Brewer various from Malt Shovel Brewery

A pub-brewery operating as an off-shoot of the Malt Shovel Brewery, a large indoor/outdoor venue where the house beers are on tap alongside a large range of James Squire and Lion Nathan brands.

Beer selection Highwayman, The Craic, Governor King

Lord Nelson Brewery Hotel

19 Kent Street, The Rocks, Sydney, NSW 2000

Tel (02) 9251 4044

Website www.lordnelsonhotel.com.au

Brewer Damon Nott

Sydney's first modern brew-pub has been brewing its own since 1987. The historic sandstone hotel has a well-run, English-themed pub with beers to match: Old Admiral is an award-winning, hearty, strong ale, while Three Sheets is a well-balanced, bitter ale with nice complexity.

Look out for the seasonal porter, Nelson's Blood. Beer-friendly pub snacks include traditional pork pies and ploughman's platter. Things can get a bit hectic on Friday nights and weekends but this place is a must for any serious beer tourist.

Beer selection Three Sheets, Quayle Ale, Victory Bitter, Old Admiral

Macquarie Hotel

42 Wentworth Avenue, Surry Hills, Sydney, NSW 2010

Tel (02) 9264 9888

Website www.macquariehotel.com

Brewer Michael Donelan

The microbrewery at this heritage-listed Surry Hills watering hole finally came on line in early 2005. The wooden-clad, 800-litre brewery is housed downstairs, though punters can keep an eye on proceedings through a clear section of floor. The cleverly named Schwartz Bier is a flavoursome dark beer, named after the pub's owner, Dr Jerry Schwartz, and is apparently based on the solitary house brew from Prague's legendary U Fleku tavern. The beer won a gold medal at the 2005 Australian International Beer Awards (AIBA). The Macquarie's beers are on tap at a handful of outlets in Sydney and Melbourne.

Beer selection Schwartz Bier, Pilsner, Pale Ale, Wheat Beer

Malt Shovel Brewery

99 Pyrmont Bridge Road, Camperdown, NSW 2050

Tel (02) 8594 0200

Website www.maltshovel.com.au

Brewmaster Dr Charles Hahn

Re-launched in 1998 as the specialist brewing arm of Lion Nathan, the Malt Shovel Brewery has built up an impressive portfolio of craft beer brands under brewmaster Chuck Hahn. (The former independent Hahn Brewery was taken over by Tooheys in the late 1980s which, in turn, became part of Lion Nathan.) By 2000, the brewery was named Best Australasian Brewery at the AIBA. The multi award-winning James Squire Original Pilsener is a richly malty Bohemian-style pilsener with few peers in the local market, while the flagship Amber Ale continues to win mainstream beer converts. In recent years, several James Squire Brewhouses have been set up as joint ventures, brewing house beers on-site to complement the James Squire range on tap at each venue.

Beer selection James Squire Amber Ale, Original Pilsener, India Pale Ale, Porter, Golden Ale

Murray's Craft Brewing Co.

Pub With No Beer Brewery, Taylor's Arm Road, NSW 2447

Tel (02) 6564 2100

Website www.murraysbrewingco.com.au

Brewer Graeme Mahy

This brew-pub newcomer located on NSW's mid-north coast first produced beer in December 2005. As the name suggests, the pub claims to be the original inspiration for the famous Slim Dusty song (a Queensland pub has similar claims). The beer selection includes a spicy Belgian witbier; an aromatic, well-bittered US-style pale ale; and a pleasantly roasty dark ale. A hugely hoppy Murray's Icon 2IPA is the latest release.

Beer selection Murray's Nirvana Pale Ale, Sunrise Wheat Beer, Swinging, Arm Dark Ale

Northern Rivers Brewing Company

57 Northcott Crescent, Alstonville, NSW 2477

Tel (02) 6628 8737

Website www.nrbrewing.com.au

Brewer Kevin Rowland

This small craft brewing operation near Lismore is run by husband-and-wife team Kevin and Andrea Rowland. Their beers are available in bottles and mini kegs from the brewery door and selected outlets.

Beer selection Northern Rivers Blonde Ale, Pale Ale

Outback Brewery

35 Dell Street, Woodpark, NSW 2164

Tel (02) 9892 4744

Website www.outbackbrewery.com.au

This tiny craft brewery is based in western Sydney.

Beer selection Country Ale, Black Opal, Outback Pilsener

CRAFTY LOCALS

Paddy's Brewery

Markets Hotel, 268 Parramatta Road, Flemington, NSW 2140

Tel (02) 9764 3500

Website www.paddysbrewery.com

Brewer Callum Service

This past winner of the Champion Small Brewery trophy (2004 AIBA), is something of an anomaly, located inside a busy 24-hour pub opposite the Sydney Markets. The microbrewery has been pumping out house beers since 2001, but VB and Toohey's New are still the pub's biggest-selling tap brands. "Something which started off as a bit of fun has got a lot bigger," hotel manager Geoff Jansen said after winning the small brewery award. "It's put us on the map." Well worth the journey to sample the house brews.

Beer selection Paddy's Amber Ale, Chocolate Porter, Pilsener, Scottish Ale

Potters Brewery

Potters Inn, Wine Country Drive, Nulkaba, NSW 2325

Tel (02) 4991 7922

Website www.pottersbrewery.com.au

Brewer Luke Scott

Potters Brewery (and Inn) takes its name from the handful of historic beehive-shaped brick kilns scattered around the property outside Cessnock. The first microbrewed beer flowed in early 2003, making it the Hunter Valley's only brew-pub among 140-odd wineries. The shiny, copper-clad, 600-litre brewing plant is in a designated tasting room, where Luke Scott conducts regular brewery tours and tastings. The house beers are available on tap and bottled in champagne bottles and magnums for takeaway sales. Hops have recently been grown on-site.

Beer selection Potters Pale Ale, Hunter Kölsch, Hunter Lager

Redoak Boutique Beer Cafe

201 Clarence Street, Sydney, NSW 2000

Tel (02) 9262 3303

Website www.redoak.com.au

Brewer David Hollyoak

Opened in mid-2004, the Redoak Cafe is the showpiece outlet for a mindboggling range of beers produced by the Redoak Brewery (which is located in western Sydney). With fruit-infused beers, chocolate-laced

J. BOAG & SON RECOGNISED AS ONE OF THE BREWING WORLD'S ELITE.

J. Boag & Son has been awarded a host of Gold Medals at the 2006 Monde Selection in Brussels, the world's most prestigious beer awards. All of Boag's core beers received a Gold Medal - James Boag's Premium, James Boag's Premium Light, Boag's Draught, Boag's Draught Light, Boag's Strongarm and Boag's St George - illustrating the extraordinary quality of J. Boag & Son's beer portfolio.

stouts and regular seasonal brews, brewer David Hollyoak has already produced more esoteric beer styles than any other local craft brewer. Inspired by European reverence for beer culture, the cafe has elevated service standards to a giddy new level. The standout house brews include Framboise Froment (featuring generous quantities of fresh raspberries) and the visually stunning Blackberry Hefeweizen. Check the tasting boards, which pair four tapas-sized dishes with different house beers. The Redoak Cafe demands multiple visits for serious beer fanatics.

Beer selection Redoak Framboise Froment, Blackberry Hefeweizen, Hefeweizen, Organic Pale Ale, Bavarian Pilsener, Vienna Lager, Special Strong Ale, Bock, Oatmeal Stout, Belgium Chocolate Stout, Belgium Choc-Cherry Stout

Scharer's Little Brewery

George IV Inn, 180 Argyle Street, Picton, NSW 2571

Tel (02) 4677 1415

Brewer Lexie Lancaster

Country publican Geoff Scharer was a man ahead of his time when he started his own pub-brewery in 1987 and refused to sell any not brewed on-site. Scharer's Lager, a traditional unfiltered Bavarian-style lager, soon became a cult item, and the George IV became a mecca for boutique beer fanciers. A strong, dark, deliciously drinkable bock followed soon after. In the early 1990s Scharer leased the Australian Hotel in The Rocks and his flavoursome beers reached a wider and appreciative Sydney market (the pub was later sold but continues to serve Scharer's beers on tap, alongside other brands). Both beers were also sold in 750ml green long-necks and mini-kegs for take-home drinkers. In early 2006, a significant era ended when Geoff Scharer sold his pub and brewery and retired from the craft beer industry. He does, however, still own the former Pumphouse Brewery which once operated in Darling Harbour. Anyone interested in buying this substantial, free-standing brewery should contact Mr Scharer (via the George IV Inn).

Beer selection Scharer's Lager, Burragorang Bock

CRAFTY LOCALS

St Arnou

Level 1, 83 York Street, Sydney, NSW 2000

Tel: (02) 9299 7720

Website: www.st-arnou.com.au

Named after Belgium's patron saint of brewing, St Arnou is a beer marketing company that has never actually owned any brewing equipment. The brands have been produced under contract by various plants; most recently, all St Arnou beers are made by Australian Independent Brewers in NSW. St Arnou's range includes a spicy Belgian-style witbier (St Cloud), a pleasantly herbal pilsener, an Irish red ale (Kildara) and the well-bittered, US-style Pale Ale. The beers are currently available only on tap in numerous outlets around Australia.

Beer selection St Arnou Pilsner, Premium Blonde, St Cloud, Pale Ale, Kildara

St Peters Brewery

15 May Street, St Peters, Sydney, NSW 2044

Tel (02) 9519 0191

Brewer Matt Donelan

Nicknamed The Lone Brewer by some in the industry, owner-brewer-distributor Matt Donelan has been joined at the tiny St Peters Brewery in recent years by his son Michael. Donelan snr bought the 600-litre microbrewery at auction and launched his Blonde brew – a pale yellow, wheat-based beer with moderate hop bitterness – in mid-2000. Initially, it was available on tap at a handful of pubs in the Newtown-St Peters area; more recently a bottled version (Green Star) has been released. Donelan has generously nurtured many new craft brewers and wannabe players over the years, and hosts a monthly real ale night at the Nag's Head pub in Glebe (first Friday, every month except January). He brews the potent Thunderbolt Strong Ale under licence for the Pumphouse Bar at Darling Harbour, and makes a range of wort-in-bag homebrew concentrates for Eastern Suburbs Brewmaker. "It's a get-rich-slowly scheme," Donelan quips, about being one of the smallest players in the craft beer market.

Beer selection Blonde, Green Star

Steel River Brewery

4 Laurio Place, Mayfield West, Newcastle, NSW 2304
Tel (02) 4960 0000
Website www.steelriverbrewery.com
Brewer Ian Partland

This craft newcomer based in Newcastle came on line in late 2005 with Pig Iron, a flavoursome tap beer that owner-brewer Partland says is a "steam beer" (basically, a lager brewed at ale temperatures). Pig Iron has a full, malty palate with a hefty dose of hop bitterness. Partland is an engineer with a background in the rag trade. Since 2000 he has run a homebrew shop in Newcastle: he took the plunge into craft brewing later, buying a 6000-litre second-hand brewhouse on the internet. He plans to roll out a bottled range called Platt's Folly.

Beer selection Pig Iron

 **QUEENSLAND**

The Brewhouse

Level 1, 142 Albert Street, Brisbane, QLD 4000
Tel (07) 3003 0098
Website www.thebrewhouse.com.au
Brewer Graham Howard

Formerly known as Aurora's, this microbrewery operates out of an upstairs bar in central Brisbane. Brewer Graham Howard is a veteran of the craft brewing scene and produces a range of beer styles made solely with Australian ingredients.

Beer selection Bulldog Cloudy Ale, Moonlight Porter, Sunshine Wheat, Star Lager, Midnight Extra Stout, Storm Real Ale, Fallen Star, Sunset Amber

International Hotel Microbrewery

525 Boundary Street, Spring Hill, QLD 4000
Tel (07) 3832 2710
Website www.internationalhotel.com.au
Brewer Rudi Herget

An inner-city Brisbane brew-pub that has recently changed hands, but is committed to continuing the house brews of the former Cheers Tavern.

Beer selection Clancy's Pale Ale, Irish Red, Indian Chief

CRAFTY LOCALS

Oxford 152

152 Oxford Street, Bulimba, QLD 4171

Tel (07) 3899 2026

Website www.oxford152.com.au

Brewer Brennan Fielding

This busy brew-pub in South Brisbane began production in early 2003 using a modified 800-litre plant acquired from the UK-based Firkin microbrewery chain. Brewer Brennan Fielding worked for the Honolulu Brewing Company in Hawaii for five years before landing on these shores in 2002. His dark Oxford Nights was the highest-scoring lager in the small brewery section of the 2005 AIBA; five regular brews are supplemented with seasonal beers including Oxford Nights, Porter and Black.

Beer selection Oxford 152, Pale Ale, Cloudy, Premium, Lite

Sunshine Coast Brewery

15 Endeavour Drive, Kunda Park, QLD 4556

Tel (07) 5476 6666

Website www.sunshinecoastbrewery.com

Brewer Jim Robinson

Situated in an industrial estate outside Maroochydore, the Sunshine Coast Brewery has been producing beer since 1998. The brewery bar has several beers on tap and the range is available in bottles for takeaway.

Beer selection Noosa Premium Ale, Sunshine Coast Bitter, Brown Ale, Dark Ale, Extra Stout

Townsville Brewing Company

252 Flinders Street, Townsville, QLD 4810

Tel (07) 4724 2999

Website www.townsvillebrewery.com.au

Head brewer Mitch Brady

Housed in a former Post Office building, this microbrewery is part of a restaurant, sports bar, nightclub and commercial kitchen complex. The house brews first flowed in 2001 and the six regular beers are supplemented by seasonals like Belgian Blonde, Annand-Ale Kölsch, Eve's Apple-wheat Beer, Chilli Beer, Brauhaus Lager and Elliot's Brown Ale.

Beer selection Townsville Bitter, Lager Lout, Burdekin Gold, Digger's Pale Ale, Ned's Red Ale, Flanagan's Dry Irish Stout

 **SOUTH AUSTRALIA**

Adelaide Hills Craft Brewing

Tel 0406 257 572

Website www.ahcb.com.au

Brewer Alistair Turnbull

This craft newcomer, located at Lobethal, is due to open in late-2006. The operation will include cellar door tastings, a restaurant and takeaway sales. An exhibition of local brewing history is also planned.

Beer selection (proposed) Pilsner, Wheat Beer, Ale

Barossa Brewing Company

Mill Street, Greenock, SA 5360

Tel (08) 8563 4041

Website www.barossabrewingcompany.com

Brewer Darryl Trinne

Housed in an 1860s wheat store, this cellar door beer maturation venture fired up in 2005. Darryl Trinne brews his beers at the Mildura Brewery and tankers the wort back to the Barossa Valley, where it is fermented and matured. Cellar-door tasting/sales are available at weekends only; beers are on tap at the local Greenock Tavern.

Beer selection The Miller's Lager, Greenock Dark Ale, Wheatstore Ale

Barossa Valley Brewing

Yaldara Estate, Hermann Thumm Drive, Lyndoch, SA 5351

Tel (08) 8524 4357

Website www.bvbeer.com.au

Brewer Stefan Walker

This new, freestanding microbrewery located at the historic Yaldara Estate in the heart of the Barossa Valley has operated since late 2005. Bee Sting is a golden, bottle-fermented ale brewed with a dash of Riverland honey and wheat malt; the slickly packaged beer is easy-drinking and moderately bittered. Partners Denham D'Silva and Fergus McLachlan previously worked in international equity finance and this is their first craft beer venture. Bee Sting is available initially in NSW (bottles only), with wider distribution planned for the future.

Beer selection Bee Sting

CRAFTY LOCALS

Grumpy's Brewhaus

115 Mount Barker Road, Verdun, SA 5245

Tel (08) 8188 1133

Website www.grumpys.com.au

Brewer Thomas Hamann

Originally opened as a homebrew shop on the outskirts of Hahndorf, Grumpy's was transformed into a brewery/restaurant in 2002 with the twin installation of a wood-fired pizza oven and a second-hand 1200-litre microbrewery from Renwick, New Zealand. All beers are available solely on-site and on tap, and show a heavy German-British influence. Regular brews include a "British/American/Australian hybrid" pale ale, a German altbier (Auld Fokker) and an unusual "pre-prohibition American pilsener" (Tom Cat) made with a hefty whack of maize. Seasonals include Smoked Porter, Oktoberfest, Honey Wheat Lager, Goldrush (Californian steam beer), Smoked Pale and Heysen Oatmeal Stout.

Beer selection Genuine Pale Ale, Auld Fokker, Red Baron, Tom Cat, Biggles Extra Special Bitter

Gulf Brewery

Website www.gulfbrewery.com.au

This brand new microbrewer is based in inner Adelaide. Gulf Brewery's beer is on tap at Old Lion Hotel, North Adelaide.

Beer selection Fish Tale Pils, Pilots Light, Humpback Pale, Kitten 9 Tails

Holdfast Brewpub

Holdfast Hotel, 83 Brighton Road, Glenelg, SA 5045

Tel (08) 8295 2051

Website www.holdfasthotel.com.au

Brewer Craig Schiller

Publican/brewer Craig Schiller installed a second-hand brewing plant in 2002 and knocks out a 500-litre batch every three weeks or so. The "three-barrel ale brewery" formerly did service in a London brew-pub as part of the Firkin chain. The beers are dispensed directly from the settling tanks and have regularly picked up AIBA medals. The most flavoursome house brew is The Dominator – a super hoppy IPA. Seasonal brews include The Dark One (a winter porter) and Strawberry Blonde (a fruit-infused pale ale brewed for summer).

Beer selection Bronze Ale, Belgian Golden Ale, The Dominator

Lovely Valley Beverage Factory

48 Main Street, Myponga, SA 5015

Tel (08) 8240 0187

A small-scale craft brewery located south of Adelaide on the Fleurieu Peninsula.

Port Dock Brewery Hotel

10 Todd Street, Port Adelaide, SA 5015

Tel (08) 8240 0187

Website www.portdockbreweryhotel.com.au

Brewer Simon Selleck

This 1883 building in Port Adelaide has a colourful history – the original hotel was closed down in 1909 by the local temperance movement and operated as a boarding house, stevedore's office and brothel until re-opening as a brew-pub in 1986. House brews include the hoppy Black Diamond Bitter; silky, sweetish Black Bart Stout (one of this country's rare "milk stouts"); and the rich and potent Old Preacher (with hints of fruitcake and mocha). In a nice touch, the latter is named after the zealous Reverend Kirby, who was responsible for having the pub closed down in the 1900s.

Beer selection Port Dock Ale, Black Diamond Bitter, Black Bart Stout, Old Preacher, Powerz Premium, Ginja

Steam Exchange Brewery

1 Cutting Road, Goolwa Wharf Precinct, Goolwa, SA 5214

Tel (08) 8555 3406

Website www.steamexchange.com.au

Head brewer Simon Fennell

Due to open for business in late 2006, this craft brewery right on the Goolwa wharf aims to be a "small regional brewery" to the south coast area, as well as a cafe/brewery door operation.

Beer selection (proposed) Steam Ale, India Pale Ale, Stout, Southerly Buster Dark Ale

 **TASMANIA**

Dark Isle Brewery

61-63 Chapel Street, Glenorchy, TAS 7010

Tel (03) 6273 7788

Website www.darkisle.com.au

Brewer Andrew Buechner

This tiny craft brewery is part of a brew-on-premise/homebrew supply business in the northern suburbs of Hobart. Bottled beers are available in selected Tasmanian outlets and a handful on the mainland. The full Dark Isle range can be enjoyed on tap at the annual Taste of Tasmania festival on Hobart's waterfront (late December to early January). Try the Belgian-inspired Triple Malt and the musky Leatherwood Porter (infused with local leatherwood honey). Dark Isle also produces Barilla Bay Oyster Stout for Barilla oyster farm/restaurant in Hobart.

Beer selection Dark Isle Triple Malt, Stout, Pale Ale, Leatherwood Porter, India Pale Ale, Brown Ale, Black Lager

Moo Brew

Moorilla Estate, 655 Main Road, Berriedale, TAS 7011

Tel (03) 6277 9900

Website www.moobrew.com.au

Brewer Owen Johnston

Probably the best-appointed microbrewery in Australia, Moo Brew was launched in late 2005 as an off-shoot of the Moorilla Estate winery, on the outskirts of Hobart. Housed in a stunning, curved, glass-and-steel building, the upper-storey brewhouse boasts sweeping views of Mount Wellington and the Derwent River. Moo Brew is a word play on Moorilla, reinforced with quirky labels designed by prominent artist John Kelly (who seems to have a thing about cows), which grace the unique, piccolo-like bottles. The initial range includes an aromatic, citrussy US-style pale ale, a promising pilsener and an easy-drinking, cloudy hefeweizen. The beers are available at the winery/brewery/restaurant and in selected outlets around Hobart and beyond.

Beer selection Moo Brew Pilsner, Pale Ale, Wheat Beer

The Two Metre Tall Company

PO Box 453, New Norfolk, TAS 7140

Tel (03) 6261 1930

Contact vertigo@2mt.com.au

Brewer Ashley Huntington

Forester Pale Ale was launched in 2003 by northern Tasmanian hop grower John Carswell, and made with his own Pride of Ringwood hops. In recent times the brand has been acquired by The Two Metre Tall Company and brewed by Ashley Huntington at the St Ives brew-pub (Huntington is negotiating to buy the microbrewery and relocate to a property in the Derwent Valley). He plans to release new brands including Huon Dark Ale and Derwent Clear Ale (all three beers are named after Tasmanian rivers).

Beer selection Forester Pale Ale

Wineglass Bay Brewing

Freycinet Vineyard, Tasman Highway, Bicheno, TAS 7215

Tel (03) 6257 8574

Brewer Claudio Radenti

This independent brewing venture run by winemaker Claudio Radenti and his partner Lindy Bull has been operating for more than a decade with various other partners involved. Their twin brews Hazards Ale and Hazards Dark were produced at the St Ives brew-pub in Hobart, though this arrangement ceased in late 2005. Radenti and Bull are currently negotiating with various operators to re-start production.

Beer selection Hazards Ale, Hazards Dark

 VICTORIA

Bell's Hotel and Brewery

157 Moray Street, South Melbourne, VIC 3205

Tel (03) 9690 4511

Brewer Josephine Horn

Veteran South Melbourne publican Bill Bell seems to have been around forever and was, in fact, born in the pub that carries his family name. Some time in the late 1980s, Bill got jack of the major breweries and installed his own tiny brewing plant, which has since been through several rebuilding stages (at one point the mash tun was an old bathtub and there are still photos of Bill splashing around in the suds). In recent years, Bill Bell has made his peace with the big beer companies, his own microbrewery has been fitted out with all the latest bells-and-whistles and winemaker turned craft brewer Josephine Horn is in charge of the brew-kettle. Bell's beers are proudly on tap next to Melbourne's best-known brews and a few of Belgium's finest. Down at Bell's pub they still barrack for the South Melbourne Swans, while Black Ban Bitter is so-named because the joint was black-listed during the fiery Formula One-Albert Park protests. Drop in for a lunchtime pint and you'll more than likely spot Bill Bell manning the taps.

Beer selection Hells Bells, Summer Belle, Black Ban Bitter, Ginger Bell, Stout Billy, Summer Lager

Bintara Brewery

Murray Valley Highway, Rutherglen, VIC 3685
Tel (02) 6032 7517
Website www.bintarabrewery.com.au
Brewer Michael Murtagh

Representing an oasis of amber nectar smack-bang in the middle of the Rutherglen wine district, the Bintara brewery is housed at the Tuileries Complex in the old Seppelt Winery. Owner-brewer Michael Murtagh is a third-generation local who is also involved in grape-growing and vineyard consultancy. Murtagh had the brewing equipment custom-made in Griffith which, at a 7000-litre brew-length, is something larger than your average "micro". The first beers were made in November 2003. Besides the Bintara range, Murtagh also produces outside brands (including O'Brien's gluten-free beer) on a contract basis. Bintara Dark Lager is probably the most flavoursome beer in the range. Murtagh says it's made with "rice flakes, oat flakes and barley flakes" in addition to malted barley, and the beer has some nice chocolate characters with a silky mouthfeel. He describes it as "a very cold-fermented dark lager" in the style of the original Toohey's Old. Bintara beers are available on tap at the brewery bar (open seven days until 6pm), while the packaged product can be bought on-site or ordered for delivery. Murtagh plans to relocate the microbrewery to his Vintara vineyard/winery in the near future.

Beer selection Bintara Lager, Pale Ale, Crystal Wheat

Bridge Road Brewers

2 Bridge Road, Beechworth, VIC 3747

Tel (03) 5728 2703

Website www.bridgeroadbrewers.com.au

Brewer Ben Kraus

Ben Kraus, at 26 one of the younger craft brewers around, set up business in "Dad's back shed" on the tourist trail in his hometown of Beechworth in mid-2005. Kraus studied winemaking at the University of Melbourne and was inspired by a couple of Margaret River microbreweries he encountered while working in the WA wine region. The wine connection extends to the pre-loved, wood-clad brewing equipment he purchased from a defunct microbrewery in SA's Coonawarra region. A "limited special licence" allows Kraus to sell from the cellar door from Wednesday to Saturday. Customers include a steady stream of tourists, plus a few locals who enjoy the novelty of drinking beer inside a working brewery. Takeaway six-packs are the most popular purchase, along with a tasting of their five beers (120ml samples). Look for the well-bittered, herbaceous pale ale.

Beer selection Beechworth Pale Ale, Dark Ale, Australian Ale, German Wheat Ale, Celtic Red Ale

Bright Brewery

Great Alpine Road, Bright, VIC 3741

Tel (03) 5755 1301

Website www.brightbrewery.com.au

Brewer David Cocks

It's been a long time between drinks, as they say – the original Bright Brewery last produced beer in 1916, but the name has been revived recently and amber nectar is flowing once more in this Victorian high country town. The re-born Bright Brewery is the brain-child of two couples – David and Julie Cocks, and Scott Brandon and Fiona Reddaway – who have all moved to Bright in recent years to raise young families. The two guys are trained engineers who, according to brewery marketing manager Reddaway, were always "mouthing off" about making their own beer. "Are you serious?" the girls challenged, and then, both being economists, they put together a feasibility study. The four friends kickstarted the venture by producing their beer at the Jamieson brew-pub but have since bought a second-hand microbrewery and housed it in Bright's main street. The "brewery door bar" includes a large outdoor seating area and makes an ideal refreshment stop for skiers en route to Mount Hotham, as well as paragliders and other visitors to the outdoors-oriented region. Bright Hellfire Ale is well-bittered with bags of chewy crystal malt character, while Blowhard Pale is more in the style of a US pale ale. The original Bright Brewery won first prize for its bottled ale and stout at the 1891 Wangaratta Show, so the 21st Century venture has a proud tradition to uphold.

Beer selection Bright Hellfire Ale, Blowhard Pale

Buckley's Beers

30 Hunter Road, Healesville, VIC 3777

Tel (03) 5962 2701

Website www.buckleysbeer.com.au

Brewer Peter Florance

Getting into the craft brewing game can be fairly straightforward, but finding an original name for the business can present quite a challenge. In 2002, winemaker Peter Florance and four buddies bought a secondhand microbrewery at auction. Florance started brewing but after two months and countless pages of possible names, the partners were no closer to a final decision. "We've got Buckley's chance of coming up with a name everyone agrees on," one of them said in exasperation ... and the name stuck. At first they made full-bodied, cloudy ales – a lager (Buckley's Pilz) followed, then a bock and, later, the odd one-off brew like Snail Pale Ale (originally created for the Yarra Valley Slow Food group). Buckley's beers can now be found in numerous outlets in Melbourne and surrounds, while the name's origin is still in doubt. Some say it's derived from "wild man" William Buckley who lived on the Bellarine Peninsula in the 19th century, others says it's a pun on Buckley and Nun, an upmarket Melbourne store.

Beer selection Buckley's Original Ale, Bitter, Dark Bock, Pilz

Buffalo Brewery

Boorhaman Hotel, Boorhaman, VIC 3678

Tel (03) 57269215

Website www.buffalobrewery.com.au

Brewer Greg Fanning

This country pub has been brewing its own for more than a decade. Publican/brewer Greg Fanning uses local spring water and produces a range of easy-drinking brews. The pub has a colourful connection with one Lily Arabella Cherry, reputed girlfriend of one of Ned Kelly's gang; her face graces the Buffalo beer labels.

Beer selection Buffalo Lager, Wheat Beer, Dark Ale, Stout

Coldstream Brewery

Corner Killara Road & Maroondah Highway,
Coldstream, VIC 3770

Tel (03) 5962 6894

Website www.coldstreambrewery.com.au

Brewer Rod Williams

Due to open in late 2006, this proposed brewery/restaurant will offer Coldstream brews on tap (plus a draught cider) and cellardoor takeaway sales. Brewer Rod Williams, who has extensive brewing experience in the UK, plans to make a continental lager, a dark lager, a real ale (served on handpump) and a traditional cider.

Grand Ridge Brewery

Main Street, Mirboo North, VIC 3871

Tel (03) 5668 2222

Website www.grand-ridge.com.au

Brewer Eric Walters

Situated in the picturesque Gippsland hamlet of Mirboo North, Grand Ridge Brewery is one of the country's more ambitious craft beer producers. Owner-brewer Eric Walters bought the defunct Strezlecki Brewery (which briefly operated on the existing site) in the late 1980s with six of his workmates; over the years he has bought out the other partners, substantially increased the brewery's output and has distributed his products to ever-widening markets. These days you can find Grand Ridge beers in most states and on tap in several cities. In recent years, Walters has taken control of the restaurant adjacent to the brewery, opened Grand Ridge Manor accommodation and even runs a Gippsland cattle property where the prime beef is raised on spent grain from the brewery (his restaurant specialises in "beer grain-fed" steak). With a wide range of beer brands, the brewery has won numerous AIBA awards (including the Premier's Trophy for Best Victorian Beer on three occasions) and can also boast Australia's strongest, locally brewed beer in Supershine (11 per cent). Gippsland Gold — a hoppy, full-flavoured pale ale — is always worth sampling.

Beer selection Grand Ridge Natural Blonde, Brewer's Pilsener, Gippsland Gold, Yarra Valley Gold, Black and Tan, Hatlifter Stout, Moonlight, Moonshine, Supershine

CRAFTY LOCALS

Hargreaves Hill Brewing Company

57 Harvey Road, Steels Creek, VIC 3775

Tel (03) 5964 6224

Website www.hargreaveshill.com.au

Brewer Simon Walkenhorst

From tickling the ivories to fiddling with fermentation – Simon Walkenhorst is a trained classical pianist who has recently turned his hand to microbrewing (or "nanobrewing", as he calls the 400-litre batches he knocks out from a shed in a remote corner of the Yarra Valley). The beer is named after Hargreaves Hill, part of the craggy ranges within Kinglake National Park that loom above the brewery. With wife Beth Williams (an opera singer) also involved in the business, the musical couple sell their beer at local markets and festivals, and have established regular outlets since kicking off in late 2004. Walkenhorst favours locally sourced ingredients (including malted barley from Powell's Maltings, Romsey) and brews flavoursome ales that are bottle-fermented (the fruity, multi-dimensional porter is a standout). Brahms and Liszt might have benefited from some of maestro Walkenhorst's libations, so might've Shostakovitch.

Beer selection Hargreaves Hill Pale Ale, Porter, Brown Ale

Holgate Brewhouse

Keatings Hotel, 79 High Street, Woodend, VIC 3442

Tel (03) 5427 2510

Website www.holgatebrewhouse.com

Head brewer Paul Holgate

Paul Holgate is not a man to rush into things. Even when he was brewing AIBA gold medal-winning ales from a shed next door to his family home in Woodend, he still had a day job in Melbourne. It was only after he and wife Natasha leased the nearby Keatings Hotel in 2002 that he finally took the plunge. By then, Holgate had built up quite a following for his beers and the pub was a natural extension for their burgeoning craft brewery. The sprawling, 100-year-old pub was thoroughly refurbished and Holgate's Bar and Restaurant opened in September 2002, their brews matched with a modern bistro menu. Immediately, real ale hounds were making the rail journey from Melbourne to sample his Bitter Pale Ale served by traditional handpump. As we go to press, there are plans to relocate the microbrewery adjacent to the pub.

Beer selection Holgate Bitter Pale Ale (labelled as Old Pale Ale in bottles), Mt Macedon Ale, Woodend Pilsner, White Ale, Porter (Winter Ale), Big Red Lager

WWW.MATILDABAY.COM

~ SAVOUR THOUGHTFULLY & ENJOY RESPONSIBLY ~

CRAFTY LOCALS

James Squire Brewhouse

Portland Hotel, 115-127 Russell Street, Melbourne, VIC 3000

Tel (03) 9654 5000

Website www.portlandhotel.com.au

Brewer Regan Palandi

This first spin-off, pub-brewery venture by Sydney's Malt Shovel Brewery opened at the Portland Hotel in 2001 and was part of parent company Lion Nathan's push into Melbourne. The 800-litre microbrewery is run as a joint-venture with the hotel which also has a range of James Squire beers on tap. Following the success of the Portland Hotel operation, other similar brewhouse ventures (co-run by Malt Shovel) have followed, such as the James Squire Brewhouse at Melbourne's Docklands precinct. The house brews can vary from batch to batch, but tend to be flavoursome, hoppy ales, unfiltered and often served directly from the maturation vessels. The Craic is a creamy, chocolatey medium-dry stout; Portland Pale is a hazy, copper-coloured quaffing ale; Speculator (when available) is an aromatic and highly bittered ale – not for the faint-hearted.

Beer selection Portland Pale, Highwayman, The Craic, Speculator

Jamieson Brewery

Eildon Road, Jamieson, VIC 3723

Tel (03) 5777 0515

Website www.jamiesonbrewery.com.au

Brewer Jeff Whyte

Jeff and Jeanette Whyte have been running the Jamieson Hotel in the heart of Victoria's high country since the late 1990s. Looking at ways to attract more tourists to their lakeside pub, they installed an attractive, cooper-clad microbrewery (bought secondhand from New Zealand) and started brewing their own beer in 2001. Their biggest seller is Jamieson Brown Ale, a classic English style with a malty, toffee-ish palate and slightly sweet finish. Their Raspberry Ale is made with fresh (or frozen) fruit from the region and based on their Pale Ale recipe – the raspberries are added five days into fermentation. The unusual ale has a nice balance of fruity, sweet and tart characters, and makes an ideal dessert beer or cleanser. Jamieson's beers are widely available in Melbourne and surrounds and the pub is part of a designated "high country pub trail", where tourists can have a "passport" stamped at each of 10 watering holes. The eye-catching Jamieson beer labels have won several awards from the Victorian Beer Label Collectors' Society.

Beer selection Jamieson Brown Ale, Pale Ale, Raspberry Ale, Mountain Ale

CRAFTY LOCALS

Matilda Bay Garage Brewery

132-142 Bangholme Road,
Dandenong South, VIC 3164
Tel (03) 9706 6589
Website www.matildabay.com
Head brewer Brad Rogers

This pioneering craft brewery began life as a tiny independent operation in Fremantle back in 1984. Matilda Bay Brewing expanded rapidly and was eventually bought out by CUB (now known as Foster's). In recent times, the parent company has re-invigorated its craft beer division and the Dandenong South brewery has become Matilda Bay's new spiritual home. The bigger-selling brands, Redback and Bohemian Pilsner, are brewed at the Fremantle brewery and Beez Neez is brewed at the Cascade Brewery in Hobart – also part of Foster's. Rooftop Red Lager and the Brewer's Reserve range (Dogbolter, Alpha Ale) are produced at the Dandenong South microbrewery (which operated as the Stockade Brewery until 2004). More importantly, the so-called Matilda Bay "Garage" Brewery is where head brewer Brad Rogers and his team tinker with new limited-edition and experimental brews. A qualified winemaker, Rogers ran the Masthead Brewery in Queensland, where many of Matilda Bay's newer brands were fine-tuned. The beer portfolio is still growing and currently includes a US style pale ale (Alpha Ale), an English bitter (Sticklers) and a Belgian saison or farmhouse ale (Barking Duck). More brands and beer styles are surely just around the corner.

Beer selection Dogbolter, Alpha Pale Ale, Rooftop Red Lager, Sticklers Best Bitter

Mildura Brewery

20 Langtree Avenue, Mildura, VIC 3500
Tel (03) 5021 5399
Website www.mildurabrewery.com.au
Brewer Stephen Nelsen

Housed in a stunning art deco building (formerly the Astor Theatre), the Mildura Brewery is pumping out sophisticated brews in the heart of the town's bustling restaurant precinct. Part-owned by local celebrity chef Stefano de Pieri and his father-in-law (and Grand Hotel owner) Don Carrazza, the 2500-litre microbrewery was commissioned in 2004, finding a ready market for its beers in the Sunraysia region. Brewer Stephen Nelsen's CV includes stints at Port Dock Brewery

Hotel (Adelaide) and Gunn Island Brewbar (Melbourne). The beer names are locally themed with the biggest-seller being Mallee Bull (a robust ale with hints of toffee and roasted nuts); other regular brews include Desert Premium (faintly aromatic, crisp, refreshing finish) and Honey Wheat (brewed with local orange-blossom honey). Check the latest seasonal and specialty brews. The beers are matched with the menu on offer at the adjacent Mildura Brewery Pub and some have been incorporated into dishes (Mallee Bull is the base for the classic chicken parmigiana sauce). Indeed, it's hard to go past the signature Mallee Bull – a big-flavoured ale to match this vibrant regional hub where the Murray River meets the outback.

Beer selection Mallee Bull, Desert Premium Lager, Murray Honey Wheat, Sun Light

Mountain Goat Brewery

Corner North and Clarke Streets,
Richmond, VIC 3121

Tel (03) 9428 1180

Website www.goatbeer.com.au

Head brewer David Bonighton

Self-styled "goat guys" Cam Hines and Dave Bonighton made craft beer hip and funky when they fired up their Richmond micro in the late 1990s. With guerilla-style marketing (they recruited members for their Goat Army) they built up an inner-city cult following for their cloudy ales and inspired a new wave of young craft brewers. Their monthly Friday open brewery nights were legendary (and always packed!) and probably paid the bills during earlier lean times. In 2005 they moved around the corner to larger premises and now hold weekly open nights, brewery tours and regular beer appreciation courses. More important, after filling countless bottles by hand over the years, they installed an automatic bottling line. Close buddies Cam and Dave proved that you don't have to brew to mainstream tastes (they've never produced a lager) and they are still the same down-to-earth guys as always. A pint of cloudy, fruity Hightail Ale drunk inside their brewery on a Friday evening is a must for any self-respecting beer lover.

Beer selection Mountain Goat Hightail Ale, Pale Ale, India Pale Ale, Surefoot Stout

Red Duck Beer (Purrumbete Brewing Company)

3551 Princes Highway, Camperdown, VIC 3260

Tel (03) 5594 7374 or 0407 526 540

Website www.redduckbeer.com.au

Brewer Scott Wilson-Brown

Scott Wilson-Brown and wife Vanessa began their brewery after they moved out of Melbourne to raise a family. Red Duck takes its name from the waddling inhabitants of Lake Purrembete, close by the brewery, which is located in the former stables of the historic Purrembete Homestead (one of the oldest homesteads in the western districts of Victoria). The brewery utilises recycled equipment, producing 500-litre batches of ale ("I don't like lager," says Scott Wilson-Brown, "I like malt-driven ales."), which are hand-bottled and bottle-fermented. A graphic designer turned craft brewer, Wilson-Brown designs his own labels and brochures. Red Duck ales are full-flavoured and include a biscuity amber ale, a robust, berry-ish porter and a take-no-prisoners strong Celtic ale.

Beer selection Red Duck Amber Ale, Porter, Golden Dragon Celtic Ale

Red Hill Brewery

88 Shoreham Road, Red Hill South, VIC 3937

Tel (03) 5989 2959

Website www.redhillbrewery.com.au

Brewer David Golding

Growing their own hops wasn't even on their minds when David and Karen Golding applied for a licence to operate a microbrewery and cafe on their Mornington Peninsula property. But, because the land was zoned "rural", they were informed that they would have to embrace some "agricultural use of land". After a bumpy six-year ride to gain their brewing licence, the first beers finally flowed at Red Hill in early 2005. Using their estate-grown hops has now become a nice point of difference, particularly when the four-metre high bines are ripening towards the March harvest. And – in a neat twist – the Goldings actually grow golding hops, along with tettnang, hallertau and willamette varieties. Family and friends are called in to help with the harvest and the hop flowers are dried at a nearby orchard's dehydrating unit. The Red Hill cafe serves tasty, beer-friendly food and the signature Scotch Ale (malty, with hints of toffee) is matched with a hearty beef pie. Other snacks include ploughman's platters, Welsh rarebit and chunks of gouda cheese served with mustard and celery salt dips.

Beer selection Red Hill Golden Ale, Wheat Beer, Scotch Ale

Rifle Brigade Pub-Brewery

137 View Street, Bendigo, VIC 3550

Tel (03) 5443 4092

This long-time brew-pub is based in a historic hotel in Bendigo, opposite the former army barracks (hence the name). It's a pleasant lunch-time stopover for travellers on the regional Victorian trail.

Beer selection Old-fashioned Bitter, Ironbark Dark, Quartz Lager, Bullion Lager, Platmans Lager, Rifle Lager

Southern Bay Brewing Company

80 Point Henry Road, Moolap, VIC 3221

Tel 1300 766219

Website www.southernbay.com.au

The former Geelong Brewery (established in 1987) has been revived recently under new ownership, name and direction.

Beer selection Bearings Draught, Bearings Light, Bearings Ale, Platinum Premium, Schonbrauhaus

3 Ravens Brewing Company

1 Theobald Street, Thornbury, VIC 3071

Tel (03) 9495 1666

Website www.3ravens.com.au

Brewer Marcus Cox

When the directors of Thornbury engineering company Zetkin discovered the delights of hand-pumped real ale a few years back (then available on tap at a certain North Carlton pub), they decided to build their own microbrewery – in a warehouse below their company offices. "When we started brewing we thought: 'If we can't sell it, we'll drink it'," says 3 Ravens/Zetkin director Zeke Yarak. After testing their wings on a tiny "pilot" brewing plant for a couple of years, they commissioned a 1200-litre microbrewery (built in Dunedin, New Zealand) and took flight in earnest in late 2005. Brewer Marcus Cox had earlier been recruited with the brief to turn their real ale dream into reality. And while the 3 Ravens directors still get through a fair volume of their own product, their bottled and cask-conditioned ales are reaching a larger audience around Melbourne. Don't miss 3 Ravens Black which has lovely licorice notes and recalls the classic English dark ale Theakston's Old Peculiar.

Beer selection 3 Ravens Blond, Black, White

University of Ballarat Brewery

Camp Street, Ballarat, VIC 3350
Tel (03) 5327 8600
Website www.ballarat.edu.au
Brewer Peter Aldred

The University of Ballarat runs brewing courses ranging from one-week short courses to three-year degrees, and students practise their craft on a 1200-litre microbrewery on campus. The brewery operates as a commercial concern producing two beers – Unigold, a lightly bittered golden ale and Dark Ale (hints of coffee and licorice) – which can be found on tap at the Eastern Station Guest House in Ballarat. "Our business is teaching, beer just happens to be one of the by-products," says Peter Aldred, a University of Ballarat food science lecturer.
Beer selection Unigold, Dark Ale

 WESTERN AUSTRALIA

Blackwood Valley Brewing Company

43 Gifford Road, Bridgetown, WA 6255
Tel (08) 9761 2204
Website www.thecidery.com.au
Brewer Mark Hollett

The range of craft beers produced here are an offshoot of the Blackwood Valley Cidery in the heart of the Bridgetown apple-growing area. The beers include a robust porter, well-bittered amber ale and an easy-drinking lager. The beer is brewed in small batches and available on tap only; free tastings are offered. There's also an on-site restaurant.
Beer selection Blackwood Bitter, Blackwood Valley Lager and Porter

Bootleg Brewery

Pusey Road, Willyabrup, Margaret River, WA 6285
Tel (08) 9755 6300
Website www.bootlegbrewery.com.au
Brewer Michael Brookes

This craft brewery has been operating in Margaret River wine country since 1994 and regularly wins awards for its hearty, dark ale Raging Bull and the fragrantly hoppy Wils Pils. Other brews include a malt-driven brown ale and a citrussy pale ale, with several rotating seasonal brews. The visitors complex features a bar and restaurant, and bills itself as "an oasis of beer in a desert of wine". Bootleg beers are on tap at a handful of Perth outlets.

Beer selection Wils Pils, Raging Bull, Tom's Brown, South-West Wheat, Settlers Pale Ale

Brew 42

Lot 114, McManus Road, Allanson

Brewer Allen Shaw

A fledgling craft brewery due to open in late 2006 in the hamlet of Allanson, 50km inland from Bunbury. The enterprise is run by three Allanson locals (Chris Martin, Allen Shaw and Andrew Pimm), partly to support their combined total of eight daughters. Four brews on the drawing board include an Irish cream stout, Irish red ale, Australian pale ale and a hoppy US-style pale ale. Proposed facilities include a tasting room and brewery door sales (minimum nine litres).

Beer selection (proposed) Moorhead, Red Tale, Buck's Bitter, Powerhouse Pale Ale

Bug Ocean Brewing Company

4-17 Minchin Way, Margaret River, WA 6285

Tel (08) 9758 7277

Website www.bugocean.com

Brewer Scott Morgan

This pocket-sized micro kicked off in March 2003, specialising in German-style beers. Its Bugs Altbier won an AIBA gold medal in 2004.

Beer selection Bugs Altbier, Hefeweizen, Kölsch

Colonial Brewing Company

265A Osmington Road, Margaret River, WA 6285

Tel (08) 9757 2781

Website www.colonialbrewingco.com.au

Head brewer Dean McLeod

This brewery, 10km from the Margaret River township, started operations in September 2003. A free shuttle bus operates between town and this brewery/restaurant, where brewery tours, tastings and takeaway sales are available. Other attractions include a sizeable children's playground, BBQ facilities and regular live music. Head brewer Dean McLeod, who worked for Sydney's Malt Shovel Brewery, says he "aims to reproduce some of the great beers of Europe". Regular brews include a Kölsch ale, an English brown ale and the full-barrelled Dr Quick strong ale (7.7 per cent); seasonals include a Belgian witbier, robust porter and a smoked rauchbier.

Beer selection Colonial Spruiker's Challenge, Pistol Whip, 18 Hands, Dr Quick

Cowaramup Brewing Company

North Leeton Road, Cowaramup, WA 6284

Tel 0404 140 607

Website www.cowaramupbrewing.com.au

Brewer Jeremy Good

A family-run operation in the Margaret River region due to open in October 2006, producing a range of ales and lagers from a new Canadian-built 800-litre microbrewery. Nine varieties of hops have been grown on-site since 2004 and facilities will include a landscaped beer garden, children's play area and brewery tours by request.

Duckstein Brewery

9720 West Swan Road, Henley Brook, WA 6055

Tel (08) 9296 0620

Website www.duckstein.com.au

Brewer Erich Massberg

Billed as "a little piece of Germany in the Swan Valley", Duckstein began life as a tiny (100-litre) brewery housed inside a restaurant. Owner-brewer Erich Massberg brewed numerous German-inspired beer styles to match the food served in the restaurant. It was the first craft brewing enterprise in the Swan Valley wine region, but has since been joined by four others. A classic Berliner weisse beer is brewed as a summer seasonal. (A second Duckstein operation is due to open at Saracen Estate in Margaret River in early 2007.)

Beer selection Munich Hefeweizen, Classic Pilsner, Holsteiner Amber, Rostocker Red, Copper Ale, Dunkel Lager

Elmar's In The Valley

8731 West Swan Road, Henley Brook, WA 6055

Tel (08) 9296 6354

Website www.elmars.com.au

Brewer Elmar Dieren

German-born couple Elmar and Anette Dieren have moved beyond a successful smallgoods shop to establish this licensed restaurant in the Swan Valley, whose centrepiece is the "only glass brewery in the southern hemisphere". The beers are brewed to the Bavarian Purity Law, served unfiltered and cleverly named: Ein Stein Pilsner is for those seeking "real intelligence" in lager; Kick Back Wheat Beer is highly topical; and Over Draft Ale is suitably well-balanced with "bankers and accountants" in mind. The restaurant site features a spacious beer garden.

Beer selection Ein Stein Pilsner, Kick Back Wheat Beer, Over Draft Ale

Feral Brewing Company

152 Haddrill Road, Baskerville, WA 6056

Tel (08) 9226 4657

Website www.feralbrewing.com.au

Brewer Brendan Varis

Another Swan Valley brewery/restaurant, whose Feral Brewing flagship White Beer can be found on tap and in bottles at numerous outlets around Perth and Fremantle. The authentic Belgian wit style is boldly spiced with dried orange peel and coriander seeds. Other brews include the fully certified Organic Pils (AIBA gold medal winner), the hybrid Feral Pale (made with German and Australian malt, British and US hops) and the creamy, chocolatey Swan Valley Stout.

Beer selection Feral White Beer, Organic Pils, German Red, Feral Pale, Monty's Mild, Swan Valley Stout

Gage Roads Brewing Company

14 Absolon Street, Palmyra, WA 6957

Tel (08) 9331 2300

Website www.gageroads.com.au

Head brewers Peter Nolin/Bill Hoedemaker

Started by two former Sail & Anchor brewers, Peter Nolin and Bill Hoedemaker, Gage Roads Brewing is a relatively ambitious venture started in mid-2005. Initially distributed in WA, the brand has been rolled

out into the eastern states (both in kegs and bottles). Gage Roads Pure Malt Lager is reminiscent of a north German lager – rich, malty and well-bittered; a mid-strength Pils and hoppy IPA are the latest additions.
Beer selection Gage Roads Pure Malt Lager, Pils, IPA

Indian Ocean Brewing Company
Mindarie, WA 6038
Head brewer Deo Lule

This brand new craft operator is due to start up at the end of 2006. Brewer Deo Lule has previously worked for the Lord Nelson Brewery Hotel, Scharer's Little Brewery and, more recently, at the Sail & Anchor.

Ironbark Brewing
55 Benara Road, Caversham, WA 6055
Tel (08) 9377 4400
Brewer Graeme White

This independent craft brewery is based in the Swan Valley region.

Jarrah Jacks Brewery
Lot 2, Kemp Road, Pembeton, WA 6260
Tel (08) 9776 1333
Website www.jarrahjacks.com.au
Brewer Greg James

Located on the Woodsmoke Estate vineyard near the timber town of Pemberton, this craft brewery is named after a legendary local bushman. The 1200-litre microbrewery opened in June 2005; its bottled beers are available at the brewery door and at selected retail outlets. Visitors can sample the range of six beers on "an authentic jarrah tasting rack" in the tasting room/restaurant. Regular brews include an easy-drinking English "session" bitter, a hoppy pale ale and a robust porter infused with local honey. Seasonal beers include a classic English brown ale and a strong Belgian golden ale.
Beer selection Jarrah Jacks Pale Ale, Settlers Ale, Best Bitter, Wheat Beer, Honey Porter

Last Drop Brewery

25 Canns Road, Bedfordale, WA 6112

Tel (08) 9497 3462

Website www.lastdropbrewery.com.au

Brewer Jan Bruckner

This brewery/restaurant is situated in Canning Vale, close to the Swan Brewery. Regular beers include a Bohemian-style pilsener, a Bavarian-style wheat beer and a full-bodied dark lager; all are available at two other Last Drop taverns and a handful of Perth outlets.

Beer selection Last Drop Pils, Wheat, Dark, Light

Little Creatures Brewing

40 Mews Road, Fremantle, WA 6160

Tel (08) 9430 5155

Website www.littlecreatures.com.au

Head brewer Simon Bretherton

Located right on the water's edge in Fremantle, this brewery/bar is a must-visit for craft beer tragics (the flavoursome beers are best enjoyed at the source, during a brewing shift, accompanied by wood-fired pizzas). Formed by several founding partners from the ground-breaking Matilda Bay Brewing Company, the 5000-litre microbrewery fired up in November, 2000. The flagship Little Creatures Pale Ale set local new standards for this style of US-inspired, highly aromatic pale ale, with generous quantities of fresh hop flowers added via a hopback device. The Pilsner is comparatively restrained and less bitter and aromatic than some interpretations of the classic Bohemian brew. Rogers' is a beautifully idiosyncratic beer – chock full of biscuit malt and floral hops, yet surprisingly quaffable and moderate in alcohol. The brewing operation has been substantially expanded recently, with packaging facilities and warehousing moved off-site.

Beer selection Little Creatures Pale Ale, Pilsner, Rogers'

Mash Brewing Company

10250 West Swan Road, Henley Brook, WA 6055

Tel (08) 9296 5588

Website www.mashbrewing.com.au

Brewer Dan Turley

Yet another new brewery/restaurant in the Swan Valley region. The restaurant – ten 250 brasserie – takes its name from the street number, and the microbrewery is a spanking new 1200-litre system, manufactured locally. The simplistically named beers include the hoppy Pale (floral and citrus notes), Haze (a cloudy hefeweizen), Black (a dark lager with coffee, chocolate and mocha notes), the easy-drinking Mex and a mid-strength "cream ale" named 50:50.

Beer selection Pale, Haze, Black, Mex, 50:50

Matso's Broome Brewery

60 Hamersley Street, Broome, WA 6725

Tel (08) 9193 5811

Website www.matsosbroomebrewery.com.au

Brewer Fiona Geraty

Matso's Cafe began brewing in 1997 but an upgraded and more substantial microbrewery started operations in 2002. The building has a colourful history, in keeping with the former pearling port's past – it was built in 1900 as a bank, subsequently operated as Matso's Store (run by the Matsumoto family), was later acquired by local property tycoon Lord MacAlpine and has been twice relocated. Matso's Broome Brewery's beers include the boldly flavoured Extra Special Bitter and the Dortmunder-style River Rocks Lager, and are available on tap around Perth. Their Cooperhead Ale is an unusual mango-infused summer seasonal.

Beer selection River Rocks Lager, Pride of Blackwood ESB, Monsoonal Blonde, Smoky Bishop Dark Lager, Pearl Dust Mild Lager

Nail Brewing

300 Murray Street, Perth, WA 6000
Tel 0413 872 337
Website www.nailbrewing.com
Brewer John Stallwood

Currently in storage and due to be relocated later in 2006, the Nail Brewery previously operated out of Bobby Dazzler's pub from 2000-2004. The flagship Nail Ale is an Australian pale ale made with Tasmanian and German hops; Nail Stout is a full-flavoured dry stout, served under nitrogen on tap. Check website for latest developments.
Beer selection Nail Ale, Nail Stout

Occy's Brewery

Newtown House, Abbey, Busselton, WA 6280
Tel 0407 991 099
Brewer Bill Annear

This new brew-pub venture, due to open August 2006, is housed in an historic building close to Geographe Bay. A wide range of beers (including seasonals) is planned, brewed in 600-litre batches and matched with a menu featuring Scotch fillet burgers, salt and pepper August whiting and creative pizzas. There is also a large, shaded outdoor beer garden with children's playground and outdoor stage.
Beer selection (proposed) Belgian Wit, Dry Irish Stout, Mexican Cerveza, Australian Bitter, Bohemian Pils, Honey Nut Brown Ale, Pilbara Pale Ale

Old Swan Brewery

3 Holmes Street, Shelly, WA 6148
Tel (08) 9211 8999
Website www.oldswanbrewery.com.au
Brewer Hugh Dunn

The original Swan Brewery riverside site was re-opened in 2001 as a cafe/restaurant and function centre with an in-house microbrewery. Master brewer Hugh Dunn, who boasts 18 years' brewing experience, conducts brewery tours and runs regular beer dinners and tastings. The house brews can be sampled from a tasting paddle and include a strongly bittered pilsener, a cloudy pale ale, a spicy witbier and a roasty porter.
Beer selection Old Swan Brewery Pale Ale, Pilsener, Porter, Witbier

CRAFTY LOCALS

Sail & Anchor Hotel

64 South Terrace, Fremantle, WA 6160

Tel (08) 9335 8433

Website sailandanchor.com.au

Head brewer Richard Moroney

This is the place where the whole Australian craft beer revolution began in 1984. These days it's part of the Australian Leisure & Hospitality company which Foster's flogged off when it was about to swallow Southcorp. Luckily, its popularity ensures that it will be business as usual – and that means lots of house-brewed beer. The IPA is a well-balanced beer, big on hop flavour, rather than over-the-top bitterness (it's also available served by hand-pump). Don't miss the chocolatey Brass Monkey Stout, a medium stout that is deliciously drinkable. The Sail & Anchor is a great place to hunker down with a tapas-style platter and watch the world go by on the pavement outside, while enjoying a few brews.

Beer selection Fremantle Pilsner, Brass Monkey Stout, IPA, Queens Special Bitter

Tanglehead Brewing Company

72 Stirling Terrace, Albany, WA 6330

Tel (08) 9841 1733

Website www.tanglehead.com.au

Brewer Allan Kelly

This brew-pub is located in the 100-year-old White Star Hotel overlooking Albany's Princess Royal Harbour. Tanglehead was one of the first beers produced in Albany back in the 1830s and the name will be revived (as an English-style pale ale) utilising a brand new, 800-litre US-built plant.

Beer selection Tanglehead, Breaksea Island Light, Deep Water Porter, Southern White Ale

Wicked Ale Brewery

Hemsley Road, Yallingup, WA 6282

Tel (08) 9755 2848

Website www.wickedalebrewery.com.au

Brewer Daniel Wind

This brewery, north of Margaret River, produces some out-there beer styles including Bad Frog Citrus Beer (flavoured with lemon and honey), a chilli beer and a dark, roasted wheat beer.

Beer selection Wicked Wheat Beer, Yallingup Old, Chilli Beer, Bad Frog Citrus Beer, Chef's Wicked Chocolate Beer

Look out for more of our great books

Kitchen Basics already in stores RRP $21.95

Written by renowned foodie writer, critic and chef Matthew Evans, *Kitchen Basics* is perfect for bachelors, out-of-home first timers and the time deprived who enjoy cooking and eating well! For anyone who doesn't know how to make perfect fluffy scrambled eggs or for those more experienced cooks who need a quick and easy mid-week meal *Kitchen Basics* is here to help.

Good Weekends Away in stores now RRP $29.95

Good Weekends Away rates and reviews 100 of the best weekend getaways, taking the guesswork and hassle out of planning your next mini-break. There are "Top 5" recommendations in everything from family-friendly properties to the most romantic getaways. Whether you want to see the sites or hideaway from the world, *Good Weekends Away* will inspire you to pack your bags and take a break.

For more information or to order please call 1300 656 052

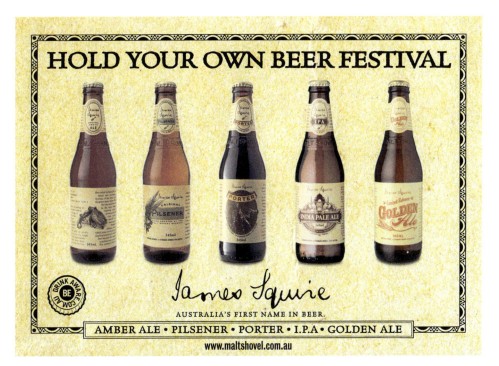

AROUND THE
WORLD IN
80 BEERS

Fasten your seatbelts and prepare for take-off. We're about to embark on an epic round-the-world journey with frequent stop-overs (80 in all) — to sample a wide spectrum of international beers now available in the Australian market.

Choosing the final 80 was not as easy as you might imagine, and we agonised over several noteworthy beers that, in the end, didn't make the cut. The general idea was to have a broad range of nationalities represented (25 countries, in fact) and also to cover as many different beer styles as we could.

Some people might argue that Germany, Belgium and England are somewhat over-represented, but these are all nations with lengthy brewing traditions and, among them, they have more than 100 different brands available in Australia. Besides, Belgium and England are the world's major ale producers — in all manner of styles imaginable — which nicely balances the plethora of lagers most other countries focus on.

Naturally, you will find many of my personal favourites among this collection of imported beers, but I include brands that display some significance beyond their flavour profile. Indeed, it would be churlish not to acknowledge a beer such as Corona (the biggest-selling imported brand in the Australian market), or the likes of Heineken and Budweiser, both of which represent a major presence on the international beer stage.

Readers should be aware that my tasting notes were made from samples that were supplied by the respective distributors. Most were as fresh as possible but, unfortunately, some consumers may end up buying the same brands only to discover they are rather long in the tooth — always seek out the freshest supply of imported beer you can lay your hands on.

And, finally, because this is not intended as a Top 80 of imported beers, I've used a rating system that reflects my personal opinion on their individual merits:

★	**some significant interest**
★★	**beer with some merit**
★★★	**recommended: a good example of the style**
★★★★	**highly recommended: well worth seeking out**
★★★★★	**a world classic**

ADNAMS BROADSIDE

ENGLAND

This malt-driven, golden-amber strong ale is handsomely packaged for export and delivers a mellow, nutty palate with a fruity, bittersweet finish. The term "broadside" refers to a naval battle manoeuvre of old, when a sailing ship would draw alongside an enemy vessel and fire all cannons on one side of the ship, simultaneously. As the nautical theme might suggest, Adnams is a seaside brewery, situated in Sole Bay, Suffolk. There is a more moderately alcoholic draught version of Broadside (4.4 per cent) in the domestic UK market, but the brewery obviously feels that drinkers deserve this all-cannons-blazing bottled ale for home consumption.

Style English strong ale

Alcohol content 6.3%

RRP $9.50 (500ml)

Distributor Vinimpex International

Contact vinimpex@optusnet.com.au

Rating ★★★

"delivers a mellow, nutty palate with a fruity, bittersweet finish"

SPAIN

The land of flamenco and bullfighting isn't renowned as a major brewing force, but a clean, malty lager like Ambar is just the thing to wash down a few tapas at lunchtime. In fact, the Spaniards have been brewing since the 1500s and a surprising number of everyday beer brands are produced for the home market (many fairly light-bodied and undistinguished, it has to be said). The Ambar brewery is located in Zaragoza, northern Spain.

Style	golden lager
Alcohol content	5.2%
RRP	$4.00 (330ml)
Distributor	Flinders Wholesale Wines
Contact	sales@flinderswines.com.au
Rating	★

"a clean, malty lager ... is just the thing to wash down a few tapas at lunchtime"

JAPAN

ASAHI SUPER DRY

Japanese brewers virtually invented the "dry beer" category in the late 1980s, using an extended fermentation process that effectively consumes residual sugars, producing a "drier" (less sweet) palate profile. Cynics might suggest that "dry" equals "less flavour" but the dry trend sparked a rash of copycat brands around the globe – including Australia, where Toohey's Extra Dry remains one of the survivors. Asahi Super Dry is relatively light-bodied with some faintly sweet notes and a short, dry finish. It's also available on tap in selected local outlets, served in a slick, frosted glass.

Style lager

Alcohol content 5%

RRP $3.90 (330ml)

Distributor Foster's Australia

Contact www.fostersgroup.com

Rating ★

"the dry trend sparked a rash of copycat brands around the globe"

BALTIKA DARK LAGER

RUSSIA

Vodka might still be the preferred tipple for most Russians but, lately, beer has been widely promoted as a more wholesome social beverage. There is also a lengthy tradition, particularly in rural areas, of making *kvass* (a home-made rye beer) that still survives in remoter parts. Before the Communist era, Russia was a major importer of English beers, particularly the strongest of stouts, which became known as "imperial Russian stouts" and were extremely popular with the Tsarist court. The copper-amber Baltika Dark Lager, brewed in St Petersburg, has some chewy caramel notes and a hint of spice in the finish.

Style dark lager

Alcohol content 5.6%

RRP $4.95 (500ml)

Distributor Merwood Wines & Ales

Contact merwoodwines@aol.com

Rating ★★

"imperial Russian stouts were extremely popular with the Tsarist court"

BATEMAN'S XXXB

ENGLAND

George Bateman & Son is a fiercely independent ale brewer from the English midlands, and XXXB is its flagship bottled brand. The term is a reminder of earlier times (before mass literacy) when casks were marked with crosses and symbols to indicate their respective strength. While not particularly strong, the copper-coloured Bateman XXXB is a deliciously complex ale with layers of malt/hop flavour, underpinned with fruity notes and a dry, dusty bitterness. The label proclaims this classic bitter as being "grainy, gristy and gratifying" – hear hear.

Style English bitter ale

Alcohol content 4.8%

RRP $9.00 (500ml)

Distributor Vinimpex International

Contact vinimpex@optusnet.com.au

Rating ★★★★

"a deliciously complex ale with layers of malt/hop flavour, underpinned with fruity notes"

BECK'S

Probably Germany's best-known brand in international markets, Beck's is relatively light in both colour and bitterness, compared with countless compatriot lagers. The brewery's proximity to the port of Bremen led it to seek export markets long before other German beer producers. Beck's is apparently the alcoholic beverage of choice for US film writer and director Woody Allen. In recent times, Beck's has been brewed under licence for the Australian market by Lion Nathan.

Style lager

Alcohol content 5%

RRP $3.20 (330ml)

Distributor Lion Nathan Australia

Contact www.lionnathan.com

Rating ★★

"the alcoholic beverage of choice for US film writer and director Woody Allen"

BELLE-VUE KRIEK

Purists might say Belle-Vue Kriek is not an authentic fruit lambic beer, but just think of it as a fun, pink, beery drink that appeals to mainstream palates. There are strict regulations in Belgium regarding lambic production, but it seems as long as a beer contains some portion brewed by spontaneous fermentation and some use of cherries, it can be labelled "lambic kriek" (the sour cherries used taste more like crab-apples than regular cherries). Belle-Vue Kriek has undoubtedly been flavoured with some form of syrup and sweetened up for modern-day tastes. It's available on tap in the specialist Belgian beer cafes throughout Australia.

Style fruit lambic (kriek)

Alcohol content 5.1%

RRP $7.60 (375ml)

Distributor Foster's Australia

Contact www.fostersgroup.com

Rating ★

"just think of it as a fun, pink, beery drink that appeals to mainstream palates"

BINTANG

Old Bali hands can fondly recall the pleasure of watching the sun set over a glittering beach with a cold Bintang close at hand. The Jakarta-based brewery was started by the Dutch colonialists and the company is still part-owned by the Heineken group. Bintang shows some hallmarks of its Dutch heritage with a solid malt content, honeyish flavour notes and enough hop bitterness to refresh a tropical thirst. The beer is the perfect accompaniment to some chicken satay skewers, dipped in spicy peanut sauce.

Style golden lager

Alcohol content 4.8%

RRP $4.00 (330ml)

Distributor Beer Importers & Distributors

Contact www.bidbeer.com.au

Rating ★

"honeyish flavour notes and enough hop bitterness to refresh a tropical thirst"

BITBURGER

GERMANY

North German lagers, like Bitburger, tend to be richly flavoured and well-bittered. This export version is noticeably less bitter than what you might enjoy in a Hamburg bar, but is still a full-bodied style of lager. *"Ein Bit, bitte"* is all the German you really need when travelling in this part of the world – these words will ensure you never go thirsty. The brewery is based in the town of Bitburg, in the heart of the Rhineland. Its flagship beer is labelled "premium pils" in the domestic market.

Style lager	
Alcohol content 4.8%	
RRP $3.30 (330ml)	
Distributor Woolworths	
Contact www.woolworths.com.au	
Rating ★★	

"Ein Bit, bitte is all the German you really need"

When the rest of the Theakston family voted to sell the famous brewery to the Scottish & Newcastle giant in the 1980s, Paul Theakston was so miffed he started his own Black Sheep Brewery right across the road in the north Yorkshire town of Masham. The copper-amber Black Sheep Ale is now one of the biggest-selling bottled ales in the UK market; it is malt-accented with some fruity complexity and hints of roasted barley. Ironically, the Theakston Brewery has been bought back in recent times by a handful of the original family.

Style pale ale

Alcohol content 4.4%

RRP $9.00 (500ml)

Distributor Vinimpex International

Contact vinimpex@optusnet.com.au

Rating ★★★

"malt-accented with some fruity complexity and hints of roasted barley"

BRAHMA

The clear glass, kinky-waisted bottle should send alarm bells ringing for any serious beer hunters: Brahma is more about style than substance. The palate is clean though thin and watery, with a low hop bitterness – but, hey, who cares when the bottle looks cute and the beer comes all the way from Brazil? Actually, Brazil is something of a sleeping giant in the brewing world: it ranks in the top six countries for beer consumption (and the producers of Brahma are a seriously large brewing company). Brahma is a relative newcomer to these shores and, obviously, another Corona wannabe in the imported beer stakes.

Style golden lager

Alcohol content 4.8%

RRP $3.50 (355ml)

Distributor Foster's Australia

Contact www.fostersgroup.com

Rating ★

"the kinky-waisted bottle should send alarm bells ringing for any serious beer hunters"

BUDVAR

CZECH REPUBLIC

Curiously, this beer brand is the subject of more international litigation than any other. It is labelled Budvar Budweiser in certain markets where the US beer giant Anheuser Busch (producer of that other Budweiser beer) hasn't successfully sued or otherwise precluded the use of the term. Alongside Pilsner Urquell, Budvar is the other great Czech beer. The brewery is located in the city of Budweis (also known as Ceske Budejovice). The legal wangling is convoluted but Budvar is straightforward enough with a mellow, malt-accented palate, faintly perfumed hop flavour and a restrained bitterness.

Style	lager
Alcohol content	5%
RRP	$3.65 (330ml)
Distributor	Beach Avenue Wholesalers
Contact	sales@baw.com.au
Rating	★★★

"a mellow, malt-accented palate, faintly perfumed hop flavour and a restrained bitterness"

An incredible amount of effort goes into brewing this beer of underwhelming blandness. For a mainstream brand, it undergoes a relatively lengthy maturation, during which time beechwood strips are added to the tanks (a traditional method of clarification which has fallen out of favour elsewhere). The so-called "king of beers" is light-bodied (a hefty portion of rice malt is used) with faintly sweet/fruity notes and negligible bitterness. Still, it's hard to argue with the world's biggest-selling beer brand — try drinking Bud early in the morning to best appreciate its subtle charms.

Style golden lager

Alcohol content 4.9%

RRP $4.40 (355ml)

Distributor Samuel Smith & Sons

Contact www.samsmith.com

Rating ★

"an incredible amount of effort goes into brewing this beer of underwhelming blandness"

CARLSBERG DELUXE

DENMARK

Carlsberg translates as "Carl's Hill" in Danish, though the brewery is located on what is more of a pimple, atop the otherwise flat city of Copenhagen. In the days of horse-drawn deliveries, it was said that the brewery's draught horses led a charmed life because they went downhill fully-laden and returned with empty barrels. It was a scientist at the Carlsberg Brewery who first identified a single strain of lager yeast that has henchforth been known as *saccharomyces carlsbergensis*. Carlsberg Deluxe is a relatively full-bodied, malty lager, well-balanced with some fruity notes and lively bitterness. It's now brewed under licence in Australia.

Style lager	
Alcohol content 5%	
RRP $3.50 (330ml)	
Distributor Independent Distillers Australia	
Contact www.independentdistillers.com	
Rating ★★	

"a relatively full-bodied, malty lager, well-balanced with some fruity notes and lively bitterness"

CARLSBERG ELEPHANT BEER

DENMARK

Visit Copenhagen during mid-winter and you'll surely appreciate the warming qualities of this blockbuster, strong lager. The robust alcohol content is matched by generous hop bitterness, resulting in a beer for sipping, savouring and basking in the lingering afterglow. This special brew is named after the famous elephant gates that guard the entrance to the picturesque Carlsberg Brewery. (Elephants are said to bring good luck.) Beware, as it's all too easy to get "elephant's trunk" on this potent number.

Style strong golden lager	
Alcohol content 7.2%	
RRP $4.20 (330ml)	
Distributor Independent Distillers Australia	
Contact www.independentdistillers.com	
Rating ★★★	

"it's all too easy to get 'elephant's trunk' on this potent number"

CHIMAY GRANDE RÉSERVE

Even by Belgian standards, this is a formidably strong ale. The dark brown beer pours with a dense, uneven ("rocky") head and the deeply complex palate shows rich toffee and spice notes (hints of nutmeg and pepper), dried fruit characters, and yet is surprisingly mellow and soft overall. Labelled Chimay Blue in 375ml bottles and Grande Réserve in the cork-stoppered, champagne-style bottle, this Trappist ale is vintage-dated (the flavour notes tend to mellow with age). With its port-like intensity, Chimay Grande Réserve is one of the world's great brews best enjoyed at about 10 degrees Celsius, with a platter of ripe blue cheese, nuts and dried muscatels.

Style Trappist ale

Alcohol content 9%

RRP $20.95 (750ml)

Distributor Beer Importers & Distributors

Contact www.bidbeer.com.au

Rating ★★★★★

"with its port-like intensity, Chimay Grande Réserve is one of the world's great brews"

CHIMAY CINQ CENTS

Chimay White (labelled as Cinq Cents in the 750ml bottle) is markedly different to the two other Trappist ales in the Chimay range. This hazy, golden-tan ale is malty, spicy and nutty at first, with citrussy notes in the mid-palate, and a dry, resinous finish, making it an ideal aperitif or a good match for seafood. Chimay White is the only Trappist beer available on tap (in selected Australian outlets) and is recommended to be served chilled. While the Chimay ales have developed a worldwide following in recent years, the monks who live in the Trappist monastery drink only a 4 per cent version of Chimay Red.

Style Trappist ale (triple)

Alcohol content 8%

RRP $18.95 (750ml)

Distributor Beer Importers & Distributors

Contact www.bidbeer.com.au

Rating ★★★★

"markedly different to the other two Trappist ales in the Chimay range"

CORONA

MEXICO

The biggest-selling imported brand in Australia is proof that some people don't actually enjoy real beer flavour. Moderate in body with some faint, grainy characters and a barely perceptible bitterness, this Mexican lager is so utterly innocuous that punters can only be drinking it for reasons of image. It's impossible to explain the remarkable sales phenomenon of Corona in purely marketing terms, but it obviously appeals to a broad range of consumers. Certain embittered critics have suggested that the wedge of lemon or lime rammed down the throat of the Corona bottle represents the only semblance of flavour.

Style golden lager

Alcohol content 4.6%

RRP $3.80 (330ml)

Distributor Foster's Australia

Contact www.fostersgroup.com

Rating ★

"so utterly innocuous that punters can only be drinking it for reasons of image"

DEUS

Deus blurs the line beautifully between the grain and the grape. It starts life as a strong, spiced ale, brewed to a giddy alcoholic strength and is then given a lengthy *methode champenoise* maturation on yeast lees, before being disgorged and corked in the traditional manner. Deus is Latin for "God" and this divine drink has set a new benchmark for style and price (it's available at only a handful of local outlets). It has the tiny bubbles (or "mousse") of a good champagne, and the dash of bergamot is a masterstroke, which would surely confuse the hell out of a bunch of wine snobs in a blind tasting.

Style strong golden ale

Alcohol content 11.5%

RRP $60.00 (750ml)

Distributor Beer Importers & Distributors

Contact www.bidbeer.com.au

Rating ★★★★★

"Deus blurs the line beautifully between the grain and grape"

DUVEL

Literally a devilish beer (the name means "devil" in Flemish), this potent, golden ale is one of Belgium's best-known specialty export brews. Duvel is lemon in colour, pours with a huge, fluffy head and is mouthfilling initially, with hints of oranges and pears and a warming, spicy aftertaste. At the Moortgat Brewery outside Antwerp, up to 13 million Duvel bottles are stored at any given time, as they undergo an eight-week maturation cycle (first in a warm cellar, then in a cool cellar). More remarkably, Duvel accounts for 80 per cent of the brewery's total production.

Style strong golden ale

Alcohol content 8.5%

RRP $7.80 (330ml)

Distributor Beer Importers & Distributors

Contact www.bidbeer.com.au

Rating ★★★★★

"this potent, golden ale is one of Belgium's best-known specialty export brews"

EMERSON'S 1812 INDIA PALE ALE

NEW ZEALAND

The original India pale ales were robust, highly hopped English beers brewed for Brits stationed on the Subcontinent, and designed to withstand the rigours of a lengthy, steamy sea voyage. Dunedin is a long way from either England or India and yet this is a brilliant modern example of the style. Brewer Richard Emerson says he uses a "potpourri" of different hop varieties to create a multi-layered palate bursting with spice, citrus and herbaceous characters, seamlessly married with bold malty notes. The name might suggest a classical "overture" of a beer, but 1812 is also the last four digits of the brewery's phone number.

Style India pale ale

Alcohol content 5%

RRP $4.95 (500ml)

Distributor Brandon Real Ale

Contact briansargent@brandonrealale.com

Rating ★★★★★

"a multi-layered palate bursting with spice, citrus and herbaceous characters"

NEW ZEALAND

This certified organic beer is breathtakingly flavoursome and really delivers on aroma with honeyish malt intertwined with floral hops and a kiss of honeysuckle. The palate has juicy malt flavours balanced with fresh, herbal hops and a lengthy afterbitterness. Brewer Richard Emerson is profoundly deaf but achieves nuances of flavour that others seem only dimly aware of. Emerson's Brewery was the most awarded (nine medals) at the 2005 BrewNZ beer awards.

Style	pilsener
Alcohol content	4.9%
RRP	$4.95 (500ml)
Distributor	Brandon Real Ale
Contact	briansargent@brandonrealale.com
Rating	★★★★★

"honeyish malt intertwined with floral hops and a kiss of honeysuckle"

This hazy, dark brown ale with ruby highlights pours with a thick, creamy head and has a heady aromatic mix featuring spice, citrus and dark chocolate. The complex palate is reminiscent of a brandy-soaked Christmas pudding with hints of allspice, cinnamon, clove, candied orange peel and dried fruit, wrapped up in a warming alcoholic afterglow. Taieri George is an annual limited-edition brew, released on March 6 to commemorate the birthday of the late George Emerson – co-founder of both Emerson's Brewery and the historic Taieri Gorge Railway.

Style spiced, strong ale
Alcohol content 6.8%
RRP $5.95 (500ml)
Distributor Brandon Real Ale
Contact briansargent@brandonrealale.com
Rating ★★★★

"the complex palate is reminiscent of a brandy-soaked Christmas pudding"

FRANZISKANER DUNKEL HEFE-WEISSBIER

A mouthful in every sense of the word – this dark tan, bottle-fermented (cloudy) Bavarian-style wheat beer is toffee-ish and creamy initially, with soft caramel and fruit notes, and a gently spicy finish. The brand was acquired by the Munich-based Spaten brewery in the mid-1800s when the beer was being produced by a nearby Franciscan abbey (hence, the jolly monk featured on the label). This is a fairly restrained interpretation of the beer style and just the thing to wash down some garlicky bratwurst and sauerkraut.

Style dark wheat beer

Alcohol content 5%

RRP $6.20 (500ml)

Distributor German Beverage Imports

Contact info@lowenbrau.com.au

Rating ★★★

"just the thing to wash down some garlicky bratwurst and sauerkraut"

ENGLAND

Complexity and balance are the hallmarks of a great ale and Fuller's ESB is one of the best going around. There is a scent of floral hops amid the dense malty aromatics, a huge malt-driven centre interwoven with luscious hop flavour notes, and a long, caramel-tinged, dusty, dry, hoppy finish. Significantly, the brewery has re-formulated Fuller's ESB in recent years and succeeded in packing even more flavour in. Rather amazingly, they have tripled the maturation time, during which the beer is dry-hopped using "hop pillows" suspended in the brew.

Style special bitter

Alcohol content 5.9%

RRP $9.00 (500ml)

Distributor Vinimpex International

Contact vinimpex@optusnet.com.au

Rating ★★★★★

"a huge malt-driven centre interwoven with luscious hop flavour notes"

ENGLAND

The delicate balance of biscuity malt flavours and a firm, hop bitterness make Fuller's London Pride an immensely drinkable ale. Like most cask-conditioned English "real ales" this beer is best enjoyed on tap, but over here on the other side of the world we have to make do with the next best thing: a bottle. Interestingly, Fuller's brew a slightly stronger version of both London Pride and ESB in bottles, believing that is the only way to replicate the fuller flavour of fresh cask ale. A pint of Pride and a pork pie make an ideal London pub lunch.

Style bitter ale
Alcohol content 4.7%
RRP $9.00 (500ml)
Distributor Vinimpex International
Contact vinimpex@optusnet.com.au
Rating ★★★★

"a pint of Pride and a pork pie make an ideal London pub lunch"

GOUDEN CAROLUS

BELGIUM

This russet-coloured, strong ale makes a wonderful dessert beer and is well-matched with chocolate flavours. The palate has a port-like intensity with hints of praline, spice and orange, and a complex, sweet-laced finish. When you think about it, that sounds like a dessert and, indeed, Gouden Carolus can be just the thing to round off a meal (without looking at the sweets menu). This funky little Belgian ale is well worth tracking down. The name means "Golden Charles" and is thought to refer to either Charlemagne or the Holy Roman Emperor Charles V.

Style strong ale

Alcohol content 8.5%

RRP $4.00 (330ml)

Importer Beer Importers & Distributors

Contact www.bidbeer.com.au

Rating ★★★★

"port-like intensity with hints of praline, spice and orange, and a complex, sweet-laced finish"

GROLSCH

HOLLAND

Groslch may be less well-known than its widely travelled compatriot Heineken, but it is definitely a more characterful lager. This rich, golden beer pours with a thick, creamy head and has a solidly malty palate balanced by a generous bitterness. The easily recyclable swing-top bottle has long been a favourite with homebrewers and sauce makers alike. Interestingly, the brewery reduced the volume from 500ml some years back to avoid a price rise; around that time, the ceramic stopper was replaced with a plastic job.

Style lager

Alcohol content 5%

RRP $6.00 (473ml)

Distributor Independent Distillers Australia

Contact www.independentdistillers.com

Rating ★★★

"the easily recyclable swing-top bottle has long been a favourite with homebrewers"

The disappointing decline in the flavour of Guinness over the past decade should be a clarion call for the anti-globalisation mob. No longer owned by Irish interests, this iconic brand has been turned steadily into a bland global commodity. The locally brewed Guinness on tap in Australia used to be a pretty good drop – full-flavoured and well-bittered – but that all changed in mid-2000 when it was re-formulated around the world to this pale imitation of its former glory. A stronger, bottled version was available for a while but, alas, that has been replaced by this imported, widget-driven contrivance. What a shame.

Style stout

Alcohol content 4.2%

RRP $3.00 (330ml)

Distributor Diageo

Contact www.diageo.com

Rating ★

"this iconic brand has been turned steadily into a bland global commodity"

HEINEKEN

HOLLAND

The benchmark among international lagers, Heineken's big break was to crack the US market straight after Prohibition ended in 1933. Ever since, the ubiquitous green bottle has become a standard in countless hotel mini-bars and upmarket bar shelves around the globe. (Naturally, it has inspired countless green bottle lookalikes over the years.) Heineken has a moderate maltiness with a hint of European hop character and a whiff of what one beer writer calls "fresh-mown hay". In recent times, Heineken has been brewed under licence in Australia.

Style lager	
Alcohol content 5%	
RRP $3.60 (330ml)	
Distributor Lion Nathan Australia	
Contact www.lionnathan.com.au	
Rating ★★	

"the ubiquitous green bottle has become a standard in countless hotel mini-bars"

HOEGAARDEN FORBIDDEN FRUIT

BELGIUM

The richly complex palate of this ale has bags of dried fruit, chocolate and spice flavours, while the finish is deliciously warming and decadent. Forbidden Fruit is spiced with coriander seed and dried curacao (bitter orange) peel, and robust enough to complement a sticky date pudding. Conversely, it can be used as an ingredient in sabayon or in a beery chocolate mud cake. The Rubens painting of Adam and Eve on the label was once considered too obscene for certain parts of the US export market.

Style spiced strong ale

Alcohol content 8.5%

RRP $5.90 (330ml)

Distributor Foster's Australia

Contact www.fostersgroup.com

Rating ★★★

"the richly complex palate of this ale has bags of dried fruit, chocolate and spice flavours"

HOEGAARDEN WITBIER

The Belgian witbier style had all but died out by the 1960s when this regional brewery was revived by local milkman Pierre Celis. Nowadays, Hoegaarden Witbier enjoys the flattery of countless imitators at home and abroad. Correctly pronounced *who-garden*, this hazy, pale lemon beer is made with malted barley, malted and unmalted wheat, a dash of raw oats and gently spiced with coriander seed and dried curacao peel. The palate is perfumed with citrus/spice and hints of honey, while the finish is slightly tart and lingering. Surprisingly, this witbier appeals to a wide range of drinkers, and is available on tap in selected outlets.

Style wheat beer

Alcohol content 4.9%

RRP $4.40 (330ml)

Distributor Foster's Australia

Contact www.fostersgroup.com

Rating ★★★★★

"a dash of raw oats and gently spiced with coriander seed and dried curacao peel"

INDIA

KINGFISHER

On the hot and dusty backpacker trail through India, a cold Kingfisher was a welcome sight that gladdened the thirsty traveller's heart (no wonder we keep ordering it back home in Indian restaurants). Sure, there are any number of lagers with more flavour, but once you've encountered a few of the subcontinent's dodgier local brews, there's no going past a Kingfisher. It shows a clean-tasting palate with some malt character and a faintly bitter finish. Kingfisher is brewed under licence across the Tasman for both the Australian and New Zealand markets.

Style golden lager

Alcohol content 5%

RRP $3.20 (330ml)

Distributor Independent Distillers Australia

Contact www.independentdistillers.com

Rating ★

"a cold Kingfisher was a welcome sight that gladdened the thirsty traveller's heart"

KIRIN ICHIBAN

JAPAN

In Japanese, *ichiban* means "number one" and this beer is made, unusually, from only the first runnings from the mashing process (much as a superior wine might be made using "free-run juice"). This deep golden lager is clean, malt-driven and relatively light-bodied (as in most Japanese lagers, rice malt is employed); the faint bitterness is almost imperceptible. Hardcore hop-heads will surely get bored mid-way through a glass, but Kirin Ichiban is probably a good foil for any Japanese cuisine where white-hot wasabi features as an accompaniment.

Style golden lager
Alcohol content 5%
RRP $3.90 (330ml)
Distributor Lion Nathan Australia
Contact www.lionnathan.com.au
Rating ★

"hardcore hop-heads will surely get bored mid-way through a glass"

KWAK

The unique, bulbous glass set in a wooden bracket is so attention-grabbing that it can sometimes distract drinkers from the fact that Kwak is a beautifully complex Belgian strong ale. The serving paraphernalia derives from olden times when such a beer might be handed up to a coachman at a watering stop for horses (and driver) – the coachman had to hold the drink in one hand while clutching the reins in the other. Kwak is richly malty with a delicious depth of flavour, showing toffee, orange and dried fruit notes, interlaced with a warming aftertaste.

Style strong ale

Alcohol content 8%

RRP $7.50 (330ml)

Distributor Beer Importers & Distributors

Contact www.bidbeer.com.au

Rating ★★★★

"richly malty with a delicious depth of flavour, showing toffee, orange and dried fruit notes"

LA CHOUFFE

La Chouffe is a red-capped gnome shown on the label and it is little folk like him who, supposedly, magically turn various secret ingredients into this ale (we think yeast might have something to do with it, as well). The brewery is set in the picturesque Ardennes region of southern Belgium and began as a tiny operation in 1982. The beer is unfiltered and pours with a huge head and lively carbonation. The palate is chockers with chewy malt and layers of spice and fruit; the finish is warming and pine-scented, with hints of orange.

Style strong ale

Alcohol content 8%

RRP $12.99 (750ml)

Distributor Beach Avenue Wholesalers

Contact sales@baw.com.au

Rating ★★★★

"the palate is chocka with chewy malt and layers of spice and fruit"

LEFFE BLONDE

Many abbeys in Belgium at one time or another produced beer, as was the case for Notre-Dame de Leffe, which had an operating brewery from the 1200s until the Napoleonic period. Sometime in the 1950s the community was apparently having financial difficulties, so a local brewer offered to produce beer the abbey could sell under its own name. The arrangement has continued under different breweries and today Leffe – the best-known Belgian abbey beer – is produced by the giant InBev group. Leffe Blonde has a complex palate with robust yeasty characters and a hint of fennel in the finish.

Style abbey beer

Alcohol content 6.6%

RRP $5.20 (330ml)

Distributor Foster's Australia

Contact www.fostersgroup.com

Rating ★★★

"many religious orders in Belgium at one time or another produced beer"

LEFFE TRIPLE

BELGIUM

The only beer in the Leffe range to be bottle-conditioned, Triple is made at InBev's Hoegaarden brewery, while the others are produced at the Artois brewery in Leuven. Leffe Triple is hazy, deep golden in colour and pours with a thick collar of foam. The palate is complex yet well-integrated, with citrus, spice and perfumed/piney notes, while the finish has hints of oak, hessian and jasmine. This is a beer that will grow on you with each new occasion.

Style abbey beer (triple)

Alcohol 8.8%

RRP $6.00 (330ml)

Distributor Beer Importers & Distributors

Contact www.bidbeer.com.au

Rating ★★★★

"complex and yet well-integrated, with citrus, spice and perfumed/piney notes"

LEFFE VIEILLE CUVEE

If their range of beers is anything to go by, the Notre-Dame de Leffe community must be a fairly well-rounded religious order. Leffe Vieille Cuvee sounds like a fine wine but is, in fact, another complex, full-flavoured, strong ale. It is garnet-coloured, with a nose that shows caramel and a hint of spice, and a veritable confection of a palate with chocolate, golden syrup, cinnamon and cherry notes, all wrapped up in a lip-smacking, warming finish. Yummo – just the thing to sip on late at night. (Leffe Radieuse is also available in Australia – also 8.2 per cent – and I defy anyone to tell them apart in a blind tasting!)

Style abbey beer	
Alcohol 8.2%	
RRP $5.90 (330ml)	
Distributor Foster's Australia	
Contact www.fostersgroup.com	
Rating ★★★★	

"the Notre-Dame de Leffe community must be a fairly well-rounded religious order"

LÖWENBRÄU ORIGINAL

GERMANY

Perhaps the best-known Bavarian lager worldwide, Löwenbräu is available in more than 70 countries and is brewed under licence in several (not in Australia, although Toohey's did make it for a brief time in the early 1980s). Löwenbräu translates as "lion brewery" and is thought to have originated from a 1300s Munich inn. Typical of the Bavarian style, Löwenbräu is big and malty, with a well-balanced hop bitterness. The famous Löwenbräu tent is a well-known landmark at the annual Oktoberfest and it's here that many Australian travellers first encounter the iconic Munich brew.

Style lager	
Alcohol content 5.2%	
RRP $3.25 (330ml)	
Distributor German Beverage Importers	
Contact info@lowenbrau.com.au	
Rating ★★★★	

"typical of the Bavarian style ... big and malty, with a well-balanced hop bitterness"

Like the legendary All Blacks on an overseas tour, this delicious dark ale is one of New Zealand's finest exports. Brewed with five different malted grains, Monteith's Black shows dark chocolate and coffee flavour notes in a well-integrated palate. The finish is silky smooth with a restrained bitterness, subtle hints of blackcurrant and blackberry, and a lingering roasty character. The Monteith's brewery still operates on the South Island's rugged west coast but many of the brands are produced at other brewing plants owned by the Dominion Breweries group.

Style dark ale

Alcohol content 5.2%

RRP $3.20 (330ml)

Distributor Liquor Source

Contact www.liquorsource.com.au

Rating ★★★★

"this delicious dark ale is one of New Zealand's finest exports"

MONTEITH'S CELTIC RED

NEW ZEALAND

This Irish red ale from across the Tasman is a bit of a wild card, but miles better than similar styles in the imported beer stakes. It is copper-tan in colour with reddish highlights and shows biscuit, toffee and Horlicks notes in aroma; the palate has a solid malt presence, with dry, roasty notes and a kiss of caramel in the finish. Monteith's Celtic Red balances enough flavour with nice sessionability and would be a fine match for some char-grilled lamb cutlets.

Style Irish red ale

Alcohol content 4.4%

RRP $3.20 (330ml)

Distributor Liquor Source

Contact www.liquorsouce.com.au

Rating ★★★

"a solid malt presence, with dry, roasty notes and a kiss of caramel in the finish"

ITALY

MORETTI LA ROSSA

This reddish-tan, strong lager is brewed in the style of a German *Maibock* (a seasonal bock usually released during May in the northern hemisphere) so it is somewhat of a surprise from the Moretti stable. La Rossa has an appetising aroma of freshly baked biscuits and a rich, malty palate with sweetish/caramel notes; the finish is quite smooth with little evidence of the substantial alcohol. The Moretti family began brewing in the city of Udine, north of Venice, in 1859, but the brewery has changed hands several times in recent decades and the beers are now produced in various locations around Italy.

Style strong red lager/Maibock

Alcohol content 7.2%

RRP $4.50 (330ml)

Distributor Arquilla Bulk Trading

Contact (03) 9387 1040

Rating ★★★

"an appetising aroma of freshly baked biscuits and a rich, malty palate"

This is a classic English brown ale from the "Geordie" heartland of Newcastle-on-Tyne but why, oh why, would you put an export beer in a clear glass bottle? Finding a fresh sample of "Newkie" Brown (one not yet affected by heat or light) is worth the effort – the dark reddish-tan ale has pleasant aromas of toffee and nuts, while the sweetish palate shows caramel, butterscotch and roasty notes; it has a low bitterness and finishes faintly sweet. Served lightly chilled, Newcastle Brown Ale can be partnered with a slice of apple pie for dessert.

Style brown ale

Alcohol content 4.7%

RRP $3.50 (330ml)

Distributor Foster's Australia

Contact www.fostersgroup.com

Rating ★★★

"Newcastle Brown Ale can be partnered with a slice of apple pie for dessert"

ORVAL

BELGIUM

There's no doubt that Orval is an acquired taste, but one well worth acquiring. Unusually, the beer is triple-fermented (the final stage is the bottle-conditioning) and pours with a surging, rocky head. The complex aroma shows yeast and pine notes; the mouthfeel is extremely "moussey" and the palate is a wild mix of pine-needle, orange and robust yeasts, with a long, dry, sappy finish (a hint of damp hessian comes from the presence of a wild yeasts). The Orval Trappist brewery makes only one style of beer, but what a brew!

Style Trappist ale

Alcohol content 6.2%

RRP $7.85 (330ml)

Distributor Beer Importers & Distributors

Contact www.bidbeer.com.au

Rating ★★★★★

"the palate is a wild mix of pine-needle, orange and robustly yeasty notes"

PAULANER SALVATOR

Potent bock beers like Paulaner Salvator were brewed by monks to sustain them during Lent, and they are still traditionally drunk during the northern hemisphere late autumn to spring period. This deep copper-coloured beer pours with a densely thick, creamy head; the nose has rich malt and syrupy intensity, while the chewy, malt-accented palate is complex and winey with a lingering afterglow of alcoholic warmth. German doppelbocks are not double the strength of ordinary bocks, but must be at least 6.8 per cent and their names end in *-ator*.

Style double bock

Alcohol content 7.5%

RRP $4.80 (330ml)

Distributor Avalon Goods

Contact www.avgs.com.au

Rating ★★★

"the chewy, malt-accented palate is complex and winey with a long, lingering afterglow"

ITALY

PERONI NASTRO AZZURRO

The Peroni family originally began their brewing operations in Milan, though these days the headquarters are based in Rome. This birra bionda (blonde beer) is pale golden with a clean, malty aroma; it shows reasonable malt weight in the palate and finishes crisp and dry. This is a lager clearly in the mould of the Heineken "export" style and, while there are more characterful European lagers around, Peroni is reliably refreshing. The brewery also makes an interesting specialty brand called Gran Riserva which is muscular and well-bittered.

Style lager

Alcohol content 5.1%

RRP $3.20 (330ml)

Distributor Combined Wines

Contact info@combinedwines.com.au

Rating ★★

"shows reasonable malt weight in the palate and finishes crisp and dry"

PILSNER URQUELL

CZECH REPUBLIC

The city of Pilsen has lent its name to the most-imitated style of beer throughout the world. The name Urquell means "source" and the original pilsener beer that appeared in the 1840s took Europe by storm. The brewery is now part of the giant SABMiller group and has been substantially modernised in recent times, but some things haven't changed – the brewing kettle is direct-fired (which caramelises and concentrates the malt flavours) and the wort is hopped in three stages with whole saaz flowers. Pilsner Urquell is rich gold in colour, malty and spicy in aroma, with layered caramel and hop flavours and a sustained bitter aftertaste.

Style pilsener

Alcohol content 4.4%

RRP $3.70 (330ml)

Distributor Lion Nathan Australia

Contact www.lionnathan.com

Rating ★★★★

"spicy in aroma, with layered caramel and hop flavours and a sustained bitter aftertaste"

RED STRIPE

Some beers, it is said, are a bit like making love in a canoe – this is one of them. Red Stripe has some subdued malt characters discernible in an otherwise featherweight body (both rice malt and maize are used in the mash) and any hop bitterness is practically subliminal. This beer will certainly quench a thirst and perhaps Caribbean revellers have access to more satisfying stimulants than the local brew. Interestingly, Red Stripe was brewed under licence for a brief time in the late 1980s by Power Brewing in Queensland.

Style golden lager

Alcohol content 4.7%

RRP $4.70 (355ml)

Distributor Diageo

Contact www.diageo.com

Rating ★

"some beers, it is said, are a bit like making love in a canoe"

Germany is often thought of as a land awash with lagers, but the brewers in the Cologne area specialise in top-fermenting beers with a soft, ale-like fruitiness, known as Kölschbier. The Reissdorf family established a brewery in 1894 and, some time after, are said to have pioneered this style of beer that other breweries in Cologne have imitated ever since. The pale golden beer looks just like a lager but has delicate fruity, leafy, scented flavour notes with little perceived bitterness, which set it apart from other beer styles. Reissdorf Kölsch is immensely satisfying and proof that not all great beers have to be blockbusters.

Style Kölsch

Alcohol content 4.8%

RRP $4.50 (330ml)

Distributor Avalon Goods

Contact www.avgs.com.au

Rating ★★★★★

"delicate fruity, leafy, scented flavour notes with little perceived bitterness"

RODENBACH

BELGIUM

Beware: this world classic can be a rude shock to the uninitiated – in fact, some first-timers complain that there must be something wrong with their beer. How could such a mouth-puckeringly tart flavour be intentional? Well, it is mainly the result of spending 18-24 months maturing in oak tuns. While Rodenbach is refreshing in an over-the-top manner, it is best enjoyed as an accompaniment to food. This garnet-hued ale has an initial sweetness and some fruity notes, but these are blown away by the acidic/tart finish (which has the faint kiss of raspberry vinegar). You have been warned.

Style Flemish red ale

Alcohol content 5.2%

RRP $6.00 (250ml)

Distributor Beer Importers & Distributors

Contact www.bidbeer.com.au

Rating ★★★★★

"how could such a mouth-puckeringly tart flavour be intentional?"

SAMUEL ADAMS BOSTON LAGER

When misguided souls say that the US is the land of bland lagers, they have obviously never tried Samuel Adams Boston Lager. This golden-tan lager pours with a vigorous, foamy collar and has a heady mix of resinous hops and toffee-ish malt in aroma. The palate is rich and thick, interwoven with caramel/toffee notes and spicy/herbaceous hops. The brew is generously dry-hopped with German hallertau and tettnang hops and – when the beer is at its freshest – their robust, resinous flavours will positively tap-dance on your tastebuds.

Style lager

Alcohol content 4.8%

RRP $4.50 (335ml)

Distributor Beer Importers & Distributors

Contact www.bidbeer.com.au

Rating ★★★★★

"their robust, resinous flavours will positively tap-dance on your tastebuds"

SAN MIGUEL PALE PILSEN

THE PHILIPPINES

Playboy magazine has a lot to answer for, not least because it once conducted a beer judging that voted this beer "the best in the world". San Mig is a pleasant enough thirst-quencher and inoffensive, in its own way, but some of us crave a little more complexity. It is pale gold, with a clean aroma and some malty notes, but lightweight in body and finishes short enough to make one wonder: where are the hops? The San Miguel group also owns the Launceston-based J. Boag & Son brewery.

Style golden lager

Alcohol content 5%

RRP $3.60 (355ml)

Distributor J. Boag & Son

Contact www.boags.com.au

Rating ★

"finishes short enough to make one wonder: where are the hops?"

SCHNEIDER AVENTINUS

GERMANY

This wheat-based double bock is strong, dark and handsome, and surprisingly easy to drink. Aventinus pours with a dense, lively head and shows aromas of licorice, espresso, banana and caramel. The palate is somewhat reminiscent of Christmas cake with raisiny, rummy, clove, allspice and cinnamon notes all wrapped up in a rich, chocolatey maltiness. Just the thing to sip while munching on a slice of fruit cake. The Schneider brewery makes several other wheat beer specialties including Edel Weisse (organic) and Eisbock (12 per cent).

Style dark wheat beer (weizenbock)

Alcohol content 8%

RRP $8.00 (500ml)

Distributor Avalon Goods

Contact www.avgs.com.au

Rating ★★★★★

"reminiscent of Christmas cake with raisiny, rummy, clove, allspice and cinnamon notes"

SCHNEIDER WEISSE

GERMANY

This bottle-conditioned wheat beer is the real deal and simply one of the best hefeweizens going around. Weisse has a cloudy, amber-tan colour with strikingly spicy, yeasty aromatics; a chewy, malty, robust palate with clove, caramel, orange and banana notes, all rolled up in a fine complexity that many other wheat beer brewers aspire to. Run by six generations of the Schneider family in Upper Bavaria, the producers claim to be the oldest brewery continuously specialising in wheat beers (since 1607).

Style wheat beer (hefeweizen)

Alcohol content 5.4%

RRP $5.80 (500ml)

Distributor Avalon Goods

Contact info@avgs.com.au

Rating ★★★★★

"rolled up in a fine complexity that many other wheat beer brewers aspire to"

SCHÖFFERHOFER KRISTALLWEIZEN

GERMANY

This filtered wheat beer caused quite a stir when named Grand Champion at the 2001 Australian International Beer Awards. It is an elegant and flavoursome interpretation of the kristallweizen style (filtered wheat beer) and has won many local fans ever since. The pale lemon beer pours with a blooming, fluffy head and shows faint banana and wine-gum aromatics. The palate has a solid malt presence, well-balanced with delicate fruity, banana and clove notes, and the finish is refreshingly citrussy. A wonderful lunchtime beer.

Style	wheat beer (weizen)
Alcohol content	5%
RRP	$5.00 (500ml)
Distributor	Beach Avenue Wholesalers
Contact	sales@baw.com.au
Rating	★★★★

"an elegant and flavoursome interpretation of the kristallweizen style"

SCOTCH SILLY

BELGIUM

Despite the name, there is nothing frivolous about this beer or the brewery, located in the town of Silly (population 1500). It typifies the sort of artisanal, farmhouse operation that was once common throughout Belgium. British ales and stouts gained a following in Belgium during both World Wars; some are still imported, while others are produced by local breweries, usually to a higher alcohol level. Scotch Silly is deep ruby-amber, with a creamy head, rich, winey/malty aromatics and a densely flavoured palate with hints of toffee and treacle. There is a hint of burnt sugar in the lip-smacking finish (a hefty whack of candy sugar – derived from sugar beet – is used).

Style Scotch ale

Alcohol content 8%

RRP $8.00 (330ml)

Distributor Beer Importers & Distributors

Contact www.bidbeer.com.au

Rating ★★★

"despite the name, there is nothing frivolous about this beer or the brewery"

SINGHA

THAILAND

Among Asian lagers, Singha is one of the most assertive. It is mouth-filling with a substantial malt hit, and has a dry, well-bittered finish that lingers for quite a while. The brewery was established in the 1930s with German expertise, and it is to the company's credit that it has continued to produce such a characterful beer. The high alcohol content and complex flavours mean that Singha can hold its own with the spiciest Thai tucker, especially fragrant coconut-milk-laced curries.

Style lager

Alcohol content 5.8%

RRP $4.50 (330ml)

Distributor Samuel Smith & Son

Contact www.samsmith.com

Rating ★★★

"mouth-filling with a substantial malt hit, and a dry, well-bittered finish"

SINHA STOUT

SRI LANKA

Now here's something completely unexpected: a potent, flavoursome stout from Sri Lanka. Sinha Stout is almost black (with some reddish hints) and pours with a dense, brown-tinged head; the nose shows dark chocolate and espresso notes, and a generous, alcoholic wallop; the palate is creamy and fat, with big mocha notes and some dried fruit (prunes), a lengthy, roasty aftertaste. This stout has as much character and ticker as Muttiah Muralitharan, that other famous Sri Lankan.

Style stout

Alcohol content 8%

RRP $4.50 (330ml)

Distibutor Beer Importers & Distributors

Contact www.bidbeer.com.au

Rating ★★★

"here's something completely unexpected: a potent, flavoursome stout from Sri Lanka"

STELLA ARTOIS

BELGIUM

Stella Artois was launched in 1926 as a Christmas beer but soon became a permanent brand and is now the stellar performer for one of the world's largest brewing companies, InBev. It shows honeyish malt and mildly spicy hops in aroma, has a reasonable malt presence in the palate, is well-balanced with delicate hop flavour and rounded off with a solid bitterness. Stella Artois is brewed under licence in various countries, including Australia, by Foster's, and New Zealand, by rival Lion Nathan.

Style pilsener
Alcohol content 5.2%
RRP $3.50 (330ml)
Distributor Foster's Australia
Contact www.fostersgroup.com
Rating ★★★

"well-balanced with delicate hop flavour and rounded off with a solid bitterness"

TAPPETO VOLANTE

A relative newcomer to these shores, this Italian import is certain to grab the attention of devotees of the full-bodied pilsener style. It pours with a dense, well-formed head and has a rich, malty aroma with a dash of spicy hops. The fullish palate is counterpointed with a pronounced, herbaceous bitterness that shows good length. Tappeto Volante means "flying carpet"; the beer is produced by a small, family-run brewery in the town of Biella, near Milan.

Style lager

Alcohol content 4.8%

RRP $3.95 (330ml)

Distributor Trumer Australia

Contact www.trumer-australia.com.au

Rating ★★★★

"certain to grab attention from devotees of the full-bodied pilsener style"

Nothing odd or temperamental about this fine English old ale – it is, in fact, named after a *peculier* (a minor church official in medieval times). Labelled as a "legendary strong ale", it is dark brown-black with reddish highlights and has a complex palate with hints of molasses, caramel and raisins, and a full, bitter finish. Significantly, dark brewing sugar is used in the recipe, rather than coloured barley malts. The brewery, in Masham, in the heart of the Yorkshire dales, was recently re-acquired by members of the Theakston family.

Style old (strong, dark) ale	
Alcohol content 5.6%	
RRP $8.75 (500ml)	
Distributor Vinimpex International	
Contact vinimpex@optusnet.com.au	
Rating ★★★★	

"complex palate with hints of molasses, caramel and raisins, and a fulsome, bitter finish"

3 MONTS

This idiosyncratic ale takes its name from the three monts (mountains) that surround the St Sylvester farmhouse brewery. Apparently, they are merely small hills, in the otherwise flat area known as French Flanders – on the French side of the border, but distinctly Flemish in spirit. An unfiltered golden ale, 3 Monts pours with a thick collar of foam, shows complex, winey aromatics and has a highly unusual palate with hints of caramel, pear skin, hessian and "barnyard", followed by a warming finish with a lingering hopsack note. Wow, quite a journey!

Style	farmhouse ale
Alcohol content	8.5%
RRP	$15.99 (750ml)
Distributor	Beer Importers & Distributors
Contact	www.bidbeer.com.au
Rating	★★★★★

"a highly unusual palate with hints of caramel, pear skin, hessian and barnyard"

TIGER

SINGAPORE

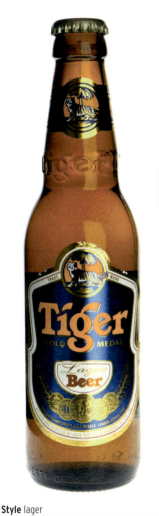

Arguably, Asia's best beer in the international lager style. The Singapore-based Asia Pacific brewery is part-owned by Heineken, and Tiger shows notable hallmarks of the parent's flagship brand. The palate has a reasonable malt content, medium mouthfeel and enough bitterness to round out what is a reliable, highly drinkable lager. Anthony Burgess wrote a novel entitled *Time For A Tiger* which reflected the beer's popularity among expat Brits in the pre-Independence colony of Malaya. A prawn laksa without a cold Tiger is like Torvill without Dean, Lillee sans Thomson.

Style lager

Alcohol content 5%

RRP $3.80 (330ml)

Distributor Lion Nathan Australia

Contact www.lionnathan.com.au

Rating ★★

"a prawn laksa without a cold Tiger is like Torvill without Dean"

TIMMERMANS GUEUZE

This is perhaps the closest thing to an authentic gueuze available in Australia. Belgian lambic beers are fermented with feral, airborne yeasts and represent a link with a medieval form of brewing. Some lambics are infused with fruit, but gueuze is a straight blend of old and young lambics; in recent times, certain breweries seem to be incorporating some standard beer to appeal to modern tastes. Timmermans version has some typical gueuze flavour notes – sour, lactic, winey, green apples, with a hint of "wet horse blanket" (indicating the presence of the wild Brettanomyces yeast). Not for everyone.

Style gueuze lambic

Alcohol content 5%

RRP $8.00 (250ml)

Distributor Beer Importers & Distributors

Contact www.bidbeer.com.au

Rating ★★★

"sour, lactic, winey, green apples, with a hint of wet horse blanket"

TIMOTHY TAYLOR'S LANDLORD

ENGLAND

Not exactly the "strong pale ale" advertised on the label, unless it means strongly flavoured and showing superb balance, with an immensely satisfying drinkability. Best drunk only lightly chilled, Timothy Taylor's Landlord is a great example of a big-flavoured beer with relatively moderate alcoholic strength. Amber-gold in colour with fresh, floral hop aromatics, it has a palate packed with juicy malt and bags of hop flavour, and a lingeringly complex aftertaste. Landlord has been named best beer at the Great British Beer Festival on multiple occasions. No wonder.

Style pale ale

Alcohol content 4.1%

RRP $9.50 (500ml)

Distributor Vinimpex International

Contact vinimpex@optusnet.com.au

Rating ★★★★★

"a great example of a big-flavoured beer with relatively moderate alcoholic strength"

TRIPEL KARMELIET

BELGIUM

The designation tripel (triple) refers to a time when breweries marked their different beer strengths with Xs and, hence, meant the strongest of three beers in a particular range. In another twist, Tripel Karmeliet is made from three different grains – barley, wheat and oats (each used in both malted and unmalted forms). The result is a beer of considerable complexity and refinement – the nose shows subtle spice/fruity notes (lemon verbena, fennel), while the palate has hints of honeyish malt, lime and perfume/spice, all melded in a deliciously tight profile.

Style abbey ale (triple)

Alcohol content 8%

RRP $8.25 (330ml)

Distributor Beer Importers & Distributors

Contact www.bidbeer.com.au

Rating ★★★★★

"the result is a beer of considerable complexity and refinement"

Some beers overwhelm the drinker with sheer flavour, while others gently seduce with elegance and finesse. Trumer Pils is almost feminine in character, with a soft fruitiness, a touch of honey sweetness and a beautifully understated hop bitterness, all delicately held in balance with a seductive drinkability. The brewery, outside Salzburg, has been owned by successive generations of the Sigl family since 1775. They insist on traditional methods – the beer is fermented in open vats and then lagered for up to eight weeks (during which time it is *krausened* with freshly fermenting beer).

Style pilsener

Alcohol content 4.9%

RRP $4.30 (330ml)

Distributor Trumer Australia

Contact www.trumer-australia.com

Rating ★★★★★

"a soft fruitiness, a touch of honey sweetness and a beautifully understated hop bitterness"

TSINGTAO

CHINA

The sleeping tiger of the brewing world has well and truly awoken: China now leads in beer production (though consumption is still a mere 20 litres a head annually). The Tsingtao brewery was founded with German/British expertise in the 1900s, which might explain why this beer has more character than other Chinese lagers. There is a hint of hop aroma, a pleasantly malty, mouthfeel and a delicate bitterness. Tsingtao makes a suitable partner for most Chinese food.

Style lager

Alcohol content 4.3%

RRP $3.00 (330ml)

Distributor Ettason

Contact (02) 9728 2288

Rating ★★

"the sleeping tiger of the brewing world has well and truly awoken"

TUSKER

Strangely, the "tusker" that inspired this brand was a charging bull elephant that killed brewery co-founder George Hurst back in 1923 (a year after the Scotsman and his brother, Charles Hurst, had established Kenya Breweries). Tusker has only recently found its way to Australia despite, apparently, being writer/big game hunter Ernest Hemingway's favourite beer. It is relatively light-bodied, with a moderate maltiness and gentle bitterness. Easy-drinking Tusker is supposedly a fine match with African peanut soup.

Style golden lager

Alcohol content 4.2%

RRP $3.50 (355ml)

Distributor Six Continents Group

Contact info@sixcontinentsgroup.com.au

Rating ★

"inspired by a charging bull elephant which killed brewery co-founder George Hurst back in 1923"

UNIBROUE FRINGANTE

CANADA

Since the early 1990s, the Quebec-based Unibroue company has been expanding its range of mostly Belgian-inspired, strong, spiced ales. In many ways, they are giving the real thing a run for its money. Fringante is a whale of an ale, with a sherbet-like mousse and complex flavour notes, including orange, fresh bread-yeast, hessian and nuts, and a deeply warming afterglow. This is definitely a late-night sipper, though the brewery produces an even-stronger specialty ale: Terrible (10.5 per cent), pronounced *terr-ree-blah* (with a French accent).

Style abbey ale (triple)

Alcohol content 10%

RRP $19.50 (750ml)

Distributor Palais Imports

Contact www.palaisimports.com.au

Rating ★★★★

"a whale of an ale, with a sherbet-like mousse and complex flavour notes"

UNIBROUE LA FIN DU MONDE

CANADA

The name translates as "the end of the world", and if it is indeed nigh – lay your hands on some of this stuff on the way out. The hazy, golden beer has a vigorous carbonation and a heady aromatic mix, featuring orange, licorice and fennel notes. The palate shows full malt, sweet honey notes and a lingering orange- and caramel-laced, dry finish. La Fin Du Monde is triple-fermented and brewed with all manner of "secret spices". It is surely enough to make the Belgians weep into their beer.

Style strong golden ale

Alcohol content 9%

RRP $7.00 (355ml)

Distributor Palais Imports

Contact www.palaisimports.com.au

Rating ★★★★★

"a heady aromatic mix, featuring orange, licorice and fennel notes"

This hazy, mahogany-coloured ale pours with a monstrous head, and shows toffee and spice aromatics. The complex flavours burst on the tongue with caramel/toffee, coriander and orange notes; the finish is notably spicy and bitter. A voluptuous ale which, like others in the Unibroue range, is bottled "on lees". The flying canoe on the label refers to a Quebec legend involving forest workers who did a deal with Satan and took to the air in bark canoes in order to spend Christmas with their families. After a few Maudites you might find yourself flying through the air without a paddle.

Style strong red ale

Alcohol content 8%

RRP $6.50 (355ml)

Distributor Palais Imports

Contact www.palaisimports.com.au

Rating ★★★★

"complex flavours burst on the tongue with caramel/toffee, spice (coriander) and orange notes"

WEIHENSTEPHANER HEFE WEISSBIER

Weihenstephan is thought to be the site of the world's oldest recorded brewery (Benedictine monks settled there in 725 AD, hops were growing by 768 and the first written reference to brewing is dated 1040). The monastery site is now state-owned and a modern brewery and restaurant operate from the historic buildings. While they make a wide range of beers, Weihenstephaner is best-known for its various wheat beers – this one is refined and very more-ish with chewy malt, delicate fruit and clove notes, and a tingling, yeasty finish.

Style wheat beer (hefeweizen)

Alcohol content 5.4%

RRP $4.80 (500ml)

Distributor Phoenix Beers

Contact www.phoenixbeers.com.au

Rating ★★★★★

"thought to be the site of the world's oldest recorded brewery"

Just pronouncing this name and style fluently will surely win kudos for any serious beer hound. There are similar German beers that make a bigger flavour bang, but Weihenstephaner Hefeweissbier Dunkel is an elegant interpretation: highly drinkable and less yeasty than others. This cloudy, copper-amber beer pours with a vigorous collar of foam and shows subtle toffee and spice notes. The palate has shades of caramel/toffee, clove and banana, melded in a symphony of flavour.

Style dark wheat beer (dunkel hefeweizen)

Alcohol content 5.3%

RRP $4.80 (500ml)

Distributor Phoenix Beers

Contact www.phoenixbeers.com.au

Rating ★★★★

"this cloudy, copper-amber beer pours with a vigorous collar of foam"

WEIHENSTEPHANER PILSNER

The state-owned brewery shares a site with the world-famous Weihenstephan university faculty of brewing (which incorporates a vast "library" of yeast strains). Access to such resource materials is an undoubted advantage to the Weihenstephaner brewers, and their Pilsner alone deserves a high distinction mark. There is a whiff of floral hops in the nose; sweet malt notes are layered in the palate and balanced by a substantial bitterness that lingers after each satisfying mouthful. Top marks!

Style pilsener

Alcohol content 5.1%

RRP $4.80 (500ml)

Distributor Phoenix Beers

Contact www.phoenixbeers.com.au

Rating ★★★★★

"sweet malt notes layered in the palate and balanced by a substantial bitterness"

WESTMALLE TRIPEL

Westmalle is one of the handful of authentic Belgian Trappist breweries. The monastery – based in the village of Westmalle, north of Antwerp – has been brewing beer since 1836. Beer was sold only in the village at first and later to a wider market. The brewery makes a "single" for the monks' own consumption, while a dark, stronger Dubbel (double) and the considerably stronger, golden Tripel are sold to the outside world. The Tripel pours with a huge, rocky head (best appreciated in a chalice-shaped glass), and the complex palate has juicy malt sweetness, spicy hops and finishes with a hefty yeasty dryness. The definitive Trappist triple ale.

Style	Trappist ale (triple)
Alcohol content	9.5%
RRP	$9.15 (330ml)
Distributor	Beer Importers & Distributors
Contact	www.bidbeer.com.au
Rating	★★★★★

"juicy malt sweetness, spicy hops and finishes with a hefty yeasty dryness"

WORTHINGTON WHITE SHIELD

ENGLAND

Worthington White Shield has been produced by different breweries over the past 100 years, as have a few other specialty English ales. The Worthington brewery was taken over by Bass in 1927, who continued to market this bottle-conditioned pale ale for 70 years until – in 1997 – it suddenly dropped the brand. White Shield has been produced since by the independent Sussex-based King & Barnes. This copper-coloured ale has a lively carbonation and a notably dry, sprucey, yeasty bitterness.

Style pale ale
Alcohol content 5.6%
RRP $9.00 (500ml)
Distributor Vinimpex International
Contact vinimpex@optusnet.com.au
Rating ★★★

"has a lively carbonation and a notably dry, sprucey, yeasty bitterness"

YOUNG'S DOUBLE CHOCOLATE STOUT

ENGLAND

This unusual stout is brewed with a double dose of chocolate ingredients – both the confectionery variety and a highly kilned malt known as chocolate malt (due to its colour). The result is a richly flavoured, yet smooth stout that appeals to sweet-toothed beer drinkers. Roasted and coloured malts can produce chocolate and coffee flavour notes in dark brews, so the inclusion of real chocolate is an obvious – though novel – step. Young's Double Chocolate Stout has hints of fudge, dark chocolate and roasty grain, with a sweetish aftertaste.

Style stout	
Alcohol content 5.6%	
RRP $9.50 (500ml)	
Distributor Vinimpex International	
Contact vinimpex@optusnet.com.au	
Rating ★★★	

"the inclusion of real chocolate is an obvious – though novel – step"

YOUNG'S SPECIAL LONDON ALE

ENGLAND

Along with Fuller's, Young's is London's other major independent brewer; both companies have reaped the benefits of concentrating on traditional ale production. Young's Special London Ale is a bottle-conditioned, copper-hued ale, with complex aromas of creamy malt and herbal, floral hops, and a multi-layered palate that features rich malt notes, fruity complexity and a lively, hoppy finish with a warming afterglow. Simply, a world classic and more characterful than a Russian novel.

Style	strong pale ale
Alcohol content	6.4%
RRP	$9.50 (500ml)
Distributor	Vinimpex International
Contact	vinimpex@optusnet.com.au
Rating	★★★★★

"simply, a world classic and more characterful than a Russian novel"

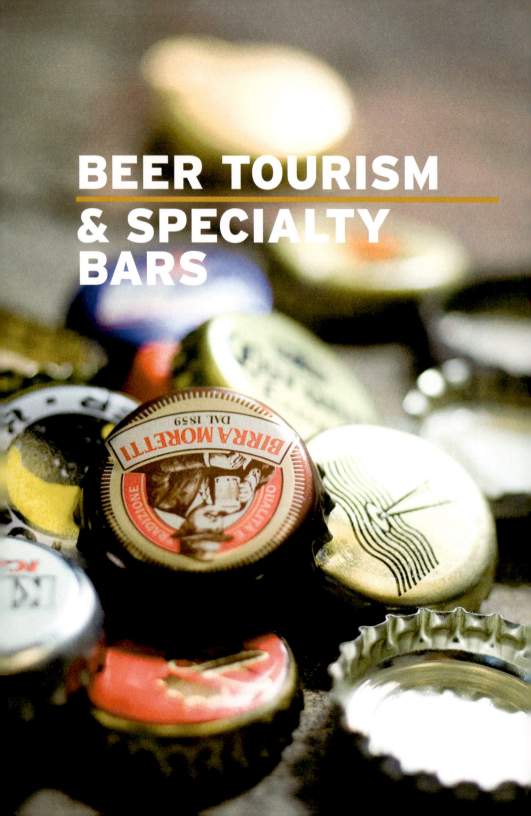

BEER TOURISM
& SPECIALTY BARS

Beer tourism is thriving, particularly in Tasmania where hordes of visitors roll up on a daily basis for guided tours through the **J. Boag & Son Brewery** in central Launceston and the historic **Cascade Brewery** in South Hobart. In 2005 more than 15,000 people visited the Boag's Centre for Beer Lovers and toured the brewing plant.

It seems there is a ready market among interstate and international tourists who want to visit the source of Tassie's pair of renowned premium lagers, partly to learn about the brewing process, but mostly to sample the beers and buy some branded merchandise or beery souvenirs to take home.

Both tours offer slightly different experiences, with Boag's plant lending itself to a more complete walk-through of the entire brewing and packaging processes. Visitors can choose between a one-hour Discovery Tour and the 90-minute Beer Lovers Tour, which includes a longer brewery tour and a sampling of King Island cheeses.

Both tours conclude with a tasting of Boag's products in the Boag's Centre for Beer Lovers, which is housed in a former pub (with a colourful past) opposite the brewery, which has been converted into a bar, shop and intimate museum. Among other items, the shop stocks Boag's "beer paper" which is handmade with a portion of spent grain from the premium lager brew.

Because the Cascade Brewery building is multi-storied and rather cramped, it's not possible to visit the actual brewhouse, but the tour makes up for that by including the in-house maltings plant (a unique feature for any Australian brewery). Keep an eye out for the maltings cat, a champion mouser who has earned his own engraved food bowl for "long service".

Naturally, the tour ends with a tasting in the visitors' centre bar which, in recent years, has been refurbished with a floor-to-ceiling window that affords a top view of the brewery's signature stone facade (while supping your favourite Cascade brew). The visitors' centre was formerly the rather stately home of the brewery manager and is in popular demand as a wedding reception venue. Take time to wander around the grounds which provide excellent angles to photograph the brewery.

For more information: Boag's Centre for Beer Lovers, 39 William Street, Launceston; (03) 6332 6300; www.boags.com.au (Discovery Tour: $18 per adult; $50 per family; Beer Lover's Tour: $25 per adult; $75 per family). Cascade Brewery Tours ($18 per adult; $50 per family), Visitors' Centre, 140 Cascade Road, South Hobart; (03) 6224 1117; www.cascadebrewery.com.au (bookings essential for all tours).

Coopers Brewery has recently started catering for beer tourism as well, offering public tours through its Regency Park facility in Adelaide. At the same time, Coopers opened a museum showcasing some of the family-run brewery's nearly 150-year history. An impressive jarrah open fermenter and various antiquated equipment on display were in use at the former Leabrook brewery until the 1980s.

Tour groups are limited to a maximum of 20 people and proceeds from the $20 fee are donated to charity.

For details contact Coopers Brewery on (08) 8440 1800 or visit www.coopers.com.au.

Many craft breweries are happy to organise tours as long as they get plenty of notice; a few offer weekly or monthly tours so it pays to ring ahead well in advance. Don't think you can just turn up and be accommodated because most of these operations are hard-working small businesses.

The **Mountain Goat Brewery** in Richmond, Melbourne, has a fully functioning bar inside the brewery, which opens every Friday night from 5pm. The microbrewery used to be housed in much smaller premises a couple of blocks away from the current site and the monthly open nights there reached legendary status. The queues to bar and toilets got ridiculously long, but the novelty of being inside a working brewery meant punters patiently waited their turn.

The superior facilities at the new Goat HQ and more regular open nights means that crowds never quite reach cheek-by-jowl levels, but they are always good fun and guided brewery tours are available (see the Crafty Locals listing for contact details).

PUB CRAWLS

One of my favourite pub-crawling precincts is The Rocks in Sydney. Within easy strolling distance via narrow laneways, zigzagging paths and a pedestrian tunnel, you can visit gorgeous old sandstone pubs, a Bavarian bierkeller, a Belgian beer cafe, a rollicking Irish-themed venue and some smart modern bars.

Taken as a whole, the compact location offers one of the most diverse ranges of tap beers available anywhere in the land. You can book an organised pub crawl – The Rocks Pub Tour, tel 1800 067 676 or (02) 9240 8788; www.therockspubtour.com – but most prefer the DIY version. Even without a map it would be impossible to get lost without stumbling upon an interesting pub or three.

Of course, the area also has its share of restaurants, designer boutiques, fine art galleries and souvenir shops, if you are that way inclined. But let's look at some of the top drinking spots in The Rocks.

Lord Nelson Brewery Hotel, 19 Kent Street; (02) 9251 4044; lordnelson.com.au. This grand old sandstone pub is the jewel in the crown of local watering holes, combining a brew-pub and well-run bar with a fine brasserie and boutique accommodation.

> Taken as a whole, the compact location (at The Rocks) offers one of the most diverse ranges of tap beers available anywhere in the land

Heritage Belgian Beer Cafe, 135 Harrington Street; (02) 9241 1775; www.belgian-beer-cafe.com.au. The stunning wooden interior of this former school hall has been transformed into a 1920s-inspired Brussels beer cafe with dozens of Belgian beers available.

Australian Heritage Hotel, 100 Cumberland Street; (02) 9247 2229; www.australianheritagehotel.com. This place specialises in Australian beer with an excellent range of local craft brews on tap, plus more than 80 bottled beers available in the unusual split-level bar.

Mercantile Hotel, 25 George Street; (02) 9247 3570. Sydney's top Irish pub. Live music and the mind-boggling quantities of Guinness served make it a favourite with the backpacker set.

Harbour View Hotel, 18 Lower Fort Street; (02) 9252 4111; www.harbourviewhotel.com.au. So close to the Harbour Bridge, you can feel the rumble of trains crossing as you sit in this smartly refurbished pub. From the rooftop cocktail bar you can watch columns of bridge-climbers making their way to the summit. The curved tile-and-brick exterior is heritage-listed.

Löwenbräu Keller, Corner Argyle and Playfair streets; (02) 9247 7785; www.lowenbrau.com.au. Lederhosen-clad waiters, foaming beer steins and traditional Bavarian fare make for a fun night out at this German bierkeller. The low, curved ceiling of this former rum bond store lends an authentic cavern feel. A good range of Munich beers on tap.

Hero of Waterloo Hotel, 81 Lower Fort Street; (02) 9252 4553. This quaintly wedge-shaped, convict-built sandstone pub is an unpolished gem from The Rocks' colourful past, and just the place to meet long-time locals.

FREMANTLE

Fremantle is essentially the cradle of the Australian craft brewing movement, where the **Sail & Anchor** (64 South Terrace) became the first modern pub to brew its own beer in 1984 as part of the pioneering Matilda Bay Brewing Company. The "Sail" is still going strong as a brew-pub.

Across the way on the edge of Fishing Boat Harbour, you can enjoy a beer poured straight from the tank inside **Little Creatures Brewery** (40 Mews Road), a working brewery/bar/restaurant. Also within walking distance is **Clancy's Fish Pub** (51 Cantonment Street) a relaxed, family-friendly pub that serves the best seafood chowder and hand-cut chips in town. It has a good range of WA craft beers on tap and in bottles, and if you happen to order a long-neck of Coopers Sparkling Ale it comes served in an ice-bucket.

When in Perth, serious beer hounds should make a bee-line to the **International Beer Shop** (69 McCourt Street, West Leederville; (08) 9381 1202; www.internationalbeershop.com), which has an exhaustive selection of imported beers (and quite a few local ones as well) plus a great range of beer-related literature, glasses and clothing.

By the time you read this, there should be up to five craft breweries operating in each of the Margaret River and Swan Valley wine regions, making both ideal destinations for a leisurely beer tour (see the Crafty Locals listing for contact details).

BELGIAN BEER CAFES

Sydney's Cafe Epoque was the first of this select chain of Belgian beer cafes to open in Australia, in 1999. Each cafe is unique but all feature Stella Artois, Hoegaarden Wit, Leffe Blonde and Leffe Brune on tap (several have Bellevue Kriek as well) and all beers are served in a rather theatrical way: glasses are chill-rinsed, filled from a generous height, sliced neatly with a "foam-cutter" and served with individually badged coasters.

The food is typically Belgian-inspired, with mussels served various ways (all with frites – the national dish of Belgium) and other classics of beer cuisine including Flemish beef stew and duck cooked in kriek.

Sydney
Cafe Epoque, 429 Miller Street, Cammeray
Cafe Heritage, 135 Harrington Street, The Rocks

Melbourne
Cafe Bluestone, 557 St Kilda Road
Cafe Eureka, 5 Riverside Quay, Southbank

Adelaide
Cafe Oostende, 27-29 Ebenezer Place, East End

Perth
Cafe Westende, Corner King and Murray streets

Brisbane
Cafe Brussels, Corner Mary and Albert streets

Canberra
Cafe Little Brussels, 29 Jardine Street

BAVARIAN BIER CAFES
The Löwenbräu Keller in The Rocks has recently spun off a pair of Bavarian Bier Cafes, with a third planned to open in 2006. With Löwenbräu, Spaten and Franziskaner beers on tap and traditional Bavarian tucker on the menu, these cafes offer a slice of Munich in the heart of Sydney.

Bavarian Bier Cafe
Shops 2-5 Manly Wharf, (02) 9977 8088

Bavarian Bier Cafe York
24 York Street, Sydney, (02) 8297 4111
www.bavarianbiercafe.com

BREW
YOUR OWN

INTRODUCTION

Homebrewing is simply one of the most practical and fun hobbies around. Like most pastimes, there are various skill levels involved but – whether you're a raw beginner or a hard-nosed veteran – there is something immensely satisfying in saying: "I made it myself."

Of course, it helps when your brew gets a mate's nod of approval, even if that entails something typically laconic like: "That's not bad." After all, those three little words can mean positively high praise when they tumble out of certain surprised mouths.

Unfortunately, many novice brewers get too easily discouraged by a minor setback, and the homebrew equipment – often received as a present – ends up packed away in a corner of the shed, never to be touched again. If you go to any suburban garage sale, I reckon there's about a 30 per cent chance you'll see a plastic fermenter or bench capper on offer – mind you, the chances of spotting some home exercise equipment are even higher!

It's a real pity because – with the right advice and some suitable encouragement – the failed homebrewer might have discovered a fulfilling hobby that also helps keep housekeeping costs down. There are plenty of specialised homebrew shops listed in the phone book and most will provide a helping hand to steer you round early pitfalls and beyond – to whatever level you want to go.

Such shops should also be able to point you in the direction of any number of websites, books on brewing and countless recipes. With luck, you might even be able to join a homebrewing club or attend a "mash" brewing demonstration.

BREW YOUR OWN

SUPERMARKET BREWERS

Backyard brewers who want to knock out the cheapest drop possible inevitably buy all their ingredients in a supermarket. That's because supermarkets can generally offer the lowest price for cans of homebrew concentrate and sugar – and that's basically all you need (apart from water) to create beer. Of course, you'll need a fermenting bucket, capper, crown seals and a few other bits and pieces, but supermarkets often carry these as well.

Hordes of homebrewers across the country are quite content to keep making beer at this basic and cost-effective level. But what supermarkets don't provide is homebrewing advice, back-up service or tips on how to improve the quality of your home-made beer.

These "supermarket brewers" can make a reasonably drinkable beer for less than 25 cents a stubbie and there's nothing wrong with that. Yet – for a few cents more and with the right guidance – they could markedly improve both the consistency and quality of their brew.

Supermarket brewers were the bane of my life when I managed a homebrew shop in Sydney some years back. Whenever they had a problem, they found our number in the Yellow Pages and rang for advice, though most of them would never end up spending a cent in the shop.

> A stick-on digital thermometer and a basic hydrometer would have solved most homebrewers' problems for a total cost of about $15.

The majority of inquiries were about whether their brew had either started or finished fermenting, or some issue concerning temperature control. A stick-on digital thermometer and a basic hydrometer would have solved most homebrewers' problems for a total cost of about $15. But when I suggested to some supermarket brewers that they should invest in these two essential items, I might as well have been trying to sell root canal therapy without an anaesthetic, such was the reaction I got.

Temperature variations are probably the biggest challenge for homebrewers. If you're operating without a thermometer, you're basically stumbling around in the dark. Similarly, a hydrometer is a fail-safe instrument for measuring the progress of fermentation; it can even help you work out the alcoholic strength of your brew.

It's not the purpose of this chapter to give detailed brewing instructions because all start-up kits and can concentrates carry such step-by-step information, but here's some priceless advice: head to your nearest homebrew shop and you'll get all the help you'll ever need.

Whenever they strike a problem, most supermarket brewers seem to turn first to "some bloke" who may or may not have known what they were talking about. I can't tell you the number of times I heard someone say: "Some bloke told me such-and-such", whenever they'd experienced a crook brew or some little problem. If your car broke down — I used to suggest to them — would you ask some bloke or take it to a mechanic? Trust me: your friendly homebrew shop should be the first port of call.

CUSTOMISING CAN CONCENTRATES

Brewing from can concentrates is a bit like heating up a frozen dinner — most of the complicated preparation and cooking has already been done for you. Standard homebrew brands usually consist of a 1.75kg can of concentrated wort, plus a sachet of dried yeast.

All you have to do is open the can, pour the contents into your plastic fermenter with some sugar or malt, add 20-odd litres of water, and stir in the yeast. Seven days or so later you can bottle your beer (with a spoonful of sugar in each bottle to kickstart carbonation) and after another couple of weeks, depending on ambient temperatures, the beer is ready to drink.

Sound easy? Well, apart from some basic cleaning and sterilising, that's really how straightforward homebrewing can be, which is why so many homies are happy to stay at this level. For other more adventurous souls, once they've mastered this entry-level brewing, they hanker after something a bit more creative, just like a home cook adding a few herbs and spices to jolly up that frozen dinner.

Apart from water, beer is essentially a combination of malted barley (or other grains), hops and yeast, and it's these three main ingredients that homebrewers can tinker with, while still brewing from can concentrates. This next stage might be called brewing with "training wheels" because you're exploring some individual freedom though the beer will still be firmly based on that reliable concentrate. In other words: it's pretty difficult to crash badly and muck up the entire brew.

BEYOND SUGAR

Any form of fermentable sugar can be converted to alcohol with the addition of yeast. Sucrose (or cane sugar) is popular with homebrewers because it's cheap, but it adds nothing to the overall character or body of the final product (in fact, beer brewed with a high percentage of sugar tends to be cidery and thin-bodied). To improve the quality of your beer instantly, simply replace the kilogram of sugar called for in recipes, with a combination of dried (or liquid) malt and dextrose.

Dextrose is derived from corn sugar and — along with the malt — will give your beer more body and complexity. Many homebrew shops sell ready-made packs of dextrose and dried malt as "half 'n' half". And, if you've got a particular commercial beer brand that you want to try to imitate, there are numerous relevant recipes available on the internet, in books or from your local brew shop.

Once you've gone beyond plain white sugar and appreciate the difference in the flavour of your beers, there's really no turning back.

INGREDIENTS

Talk about a kid in a candy store — whenever I find myself inside a brewing supply shop I can't help scanning the shelves lined with can concentrates, examining the pre-packed bags of different grains and hops and the various brewing paraphernalia. Some people might look around such a store and just see rather plainly packaged ingredients and practical bits of equipment, but I see heaps of potential beer — lovely, flavoursome, hoppy and home-made. Bring it on!

> Rubbing a single hop flower or pellet between your palms and inhaling the aroma can be a magical experience, as each variety gives up its unique spicy, citrussy or floral characteristics.

Many homebrewers develop what might be called "hop head syndrome", and no wonder. Hops are basically the seasoning in beer and can contribute different degrees of aroma, flavour and bitterness, depending on how they are employed. Rubbing varieties of a single hop flower or pellet between your palms and inhaling the aroma can be a magical experience, as each gives up its unique spicy, citrussy or floral characteristics.

Most commercial breweries employ hops for bitterness only, generally using a bulk form of liquid hop extract to produce beers of relatively moderate bitterness. Dealing with the raw ingredient can be a heady experience and — while it's easy to see why some homebrewers might get carried away — there's another sound reason why they get heavy-handed with hops.

The taste profile of any beer is all about perceived flavours. Commercial mainstream beers are generally lighter-bodied and less complex, so that even a moderate bitterness is apparent to the taster. When homebrewers start to use malt and dextrose, they are making fuller-flavoured and fuller-bodied beers which can effectively be matched by a bolder form of hoppiness.

Once you've found a combination of concentrate, dextrose and malt that results in a beer that you're happy with, it may be time to experiment with hops. Bring 500ml or so of water to the boil in a saucepan, switch off and stir in 20g of hop pellets (golding for ales, saaz for lagers is a good starting point). Let this "hop tea" steep for about 15 minutes and then simply strain it into the fermenter along with the concentrate and water, as per a normal brew.

This moderate amount of hopping will add a new flavour note to your beer, without changing the overall bitterness. Once you get hooked on such customising techniques, the sky's the limit. Soon you'll be on the road to becoming a full grain or mash brewer.

> While hops provide the condiments for beer, malted barley is the heart and soul of the amber nectar.

While hops provide the condiments for beer, malted barley is the heart and soul of the amber nectar (with the addition of malted wheat, in the case of wheat beers). It's also possible to customise can concentrates with some different specialty malted grains which, again, will provide a convenient stepping stone to brewing entirely with grains. You can even do a "mini mash" using a kilogram of pale malted barley instead of the dextrose/malt combo (ask at your local shop for guidance).

SHORT-CUTS TO HIGHER QUALITY

If you want to ramp up the quality of your brew without bothering with these customising steps, there are a couple of options at hand. Some homebrew wholesalers carry lines of liquid wort in various beer styles. Eastern Suburbs Brewmaker in Sydney offers a range produced by the tiny St Peters craft brewery.

These liquid worts are packed in large plastic jerry cans and are basically brewery-fresh wort that has been cooled and packed. All you have to do is tip the contents into a fermenter, top up with water and pitch the yeast, as instructed. The liquid worts work out a little more expensive than brewing with concentrates and additives, but the resulting beer reflects the higher quality, and with even less effort and preparation required from you.

Another route to pursue — particularly for those who would like to homebrew but are pushed for spare time or space — is to seek out a brew-on-premises shop. These places provide all the recipes, ingredients, equipment and space required — you just go in and brew, then return to bottle your own beer through an automated, foolproof system.

Bottling is one part of the homebrewing regime that seems to wear people down, particularly the necessary cleaning, sterilising and rinsing routine. If you get sick of washing bottles, it's probably time to splash out on a draught beer system at home.

You'll need some old soft drink kegs (the 18-litre variety is ideal), gas and beer lines, a regulator, a gas bottle, a beer tap or gun, and an old fridge to accommodate the whole set-up.

Most homebrew shops will provide the entire package (apart from the fridge) for around $450. Serving your own beer on tap at home has plenty of appeal, especially when it means you can throw most of your bottles away.

MASH BREWING

Full grain or mash brewing is the ultimate stage for the homebrewer, but it certainly isn't for everyone. Mash brewers are definitely not trying to produce cheap beer and they pretty much need a full mini-brewery set-up. However, once they've got the necessary equipment in place, the cost of raw ingredients can work out at even less than brewing with can concentrate.

Brewing from scratch involves several distinct stages, each requiring specialised equipment, plus a healthy time commitment (about five to six hours from start to finish). I'd advise anyone vaguely considering taking up mash brewing to watch someone else going through the entire process first before jumping in.

We ran regular weekend mash brewing demonstrations at the shop I used to run and it worked well — about half the observers went on to the mash level, while the rest realised the level of commitment just wasn't for them. Those who embraced mash brewing inevitably found an extremely fulfilling hobby and a new appreciation for hand-crafted beer.

BREWING NOTES

BEER
SOMMELIER'S
HANDBOOK

INTRODUCTION

Imagine visiting your favourite restaurant and being able to call on the services of a beer sommelier. You inform him (or her) that you and your dining companion want to drink beer throughout the meal and ask for their suggestions.

"Certainly, sir," the beer sommelier beams. "Might I recommend the hand-pumped English bitter to begin with? We've just tapped a new cask and it's pouring as clear as a bell. And, for madam, perhaps a flute of kriek or framboise, as an aperitif."

As you relax with your pre-dinner beer, the sommelier runs through various recommendations to accompany the dishes you have ordered.

"With the seafood risotto, I would suggest the Belgian wit. And for your oysters, sir, we have some aged Coopers Stout or imported Guinness Foreign Extra Stout, or you might prefer one of our locally brewed pilseners. With mains, you might like a red lager or an amber ale with the duck, and the German rauch bier is fantastic with the smoked chicken caesar salad. If you were thinking of ordering the cheese board later, we have a new batch of barley wine, as well as several vintages of Chimay Grande Réserve and some excellent strong ales."

This is pure fantasy, of course, but a worthy pipe-dream for any beer lover who's heartily sick of wine snobbism and elitism. Why shouldn't beer be treated with the same seriousness and reverence as wine? At very least, why shouldn't we expect a sound level of informed product knowledge from the people who serve beer in our bars and restaurants? Bring on the beer sommeliers, I reckon.

Wine sommeliers are now commonplace in fine-dining restaurants. Some are merely head wine waiters and more than a few have jeroboam-sized egos, which supposedly comes with their vast wine knowledge. Other waitstaff will often defer to the sommelier when a customer queries a supposedly cork-tainted or oxidised wine, or for specialised information or wine recommendations.

When I visited the Trumer brewery, outside Salzburg, Austria, I was delighted to discover that the brewmaster, Alex Kiesbye, regularly conducts a beer sommelier course. The 10-day course comprises 100 individual teaching units covering everything from international brewing methods, draught beer technology, designing a beer menu, cooking with beer and matching beer with food.

Thirty per cent of the course involves practical work, with participants working for a day in the Trumer brewery, making their own beer on a tiny pilot plant and tasting different beer styles (including "spoilt beer"). Graduates of the beer sommelier course include amateur beer lovers, hospitality teachers, bar and restaurant owners, serving staff, brewers, beer sales people and journalists.

Trumer Pils is an outstanding beer: in 2004, at an independent brewery competition held in Germany, it beat a field of 50 European pilseners to win its category. The company obviously feels that educating people generally about beer will improve the appreciation for its fine products. What a pity an Australian brewery hasn't come up with a similar concept.

My dictionary says a sommelier is "a specialised waiter responsible for serving wine, as well as offering advice on specific food and wine combinations". Wondering where the term originated, I consulted a couple of my wine-writing colleagues. It drew a blank except for the suggestion that it was probably derived from French. I asked more wine writers and drew more blanks – they simply shrugged shoulders and generally didn't have a clue.

My trusty computer search engine led me to a surprising discovery: sommelier is derived from an old French word *sommier* meaning "pack animal" or "beast of burden". Perhaps the original sommeliers were simply boofy blokes who were despatched to the cellar to fetch a new wine barrel which, needless to say, they would have sampled first to ensure that the wine was unspoilt and fit to drink.

It's a rather humble origin for what has evolved into a lofty modern-day job, so next time a wine sommelier gets a bit uppity you might remind him (or her) that they are little more than a donkey designed to transport wine to your table!

STRONGEST LINK

We should never overlook the fact that bartenders and waitstaff are the last but most important link in the beer chain. In the final analysis, it really doesn't matter how good the brewer is or how much money was spent renovating the bar, if the bartender gets it wrong, the bar may well lose a customer forever.

Pouring beer is one thing – and we'll get to that in a moment – but there are all sorts of ways that hospitality staff can sabotage what should be a pleasant social occasion. For starters, they might stuff up the order and pour the wrong beer, or they might bring too much attitude to work and forget that, after all, their job is to serve customers. (That doesn't mean being servile but it does mean they should at least give the appearance of caring about customers' needs.)

The best operators in the pub, bar and restaurant game generally realise that waitstaff are both their most precious resource and their greatest liability. Train your staff well and do it often, is the often-heard catch cry, especially as staff turnover rates are notoriously high in the hospitality industry. Moreover, think about ways to motivate your long-term staff so they become your best trainers.

Occasionally, I get approached to design a beer-list and write tasting notes for a bar or restaurant. Whenever I have agreed to do such work, it's always on the basis that I can conduct a follow-up staff training session. Let's face it, it's pointless having a great beer selection and comprehensive (and, sometimes, wittily written) tasting notes if the people who actually serve the beer aren't included in the overall package.

They are the ones, after all, who should be suggesting beers to certain customers and, hopefully, are able to describe the different styles and where the beers come from. These are the basic things you would expect when ordering wine, so why should it be any different for beer?

First, I explain to the staff why I chose certain beers and talk about the balance of various styles which make up the beer-list. Some of the more unusual beers might never become big sellers, but they are on the list for the discerning customer or for that special occasion.

I get the staff to run through their normal pouring and serving regime, and then add my own suggestions. Some of the stronger beers require a different pouring technique – which I demonstrate – and we look at the individual glasses that are often supplied by the distributors.

Then we get to the really enjoyable part: the beer tasting! I usually choose six or so beers from the list and I always include a couple of the more esoteric brews – perhaps a cherry-infused kriek or a

Trappist ale – because I really want to push the envelope of people's expectations of what a beer can be. Ideally, the staff discover a personal "favourite" from the line-up, which they will enthusiastically recommend to customers and, funnily enough, it becomes one of the establishment's biggest sellers.

Conducting a training session like that is all very well, but you really need to instil an ongoing commitment to beer appreciation and enthusiasm for the beer-list. I encourage the staff to sample every beer on the list (perhaps a different one at the end of each shift) and suggest to management that they hold monthly beer tasting sessions.

> There are all sorts of ways that hospitality staff can sabotage what should be a pleasant social occasion

Try to make these sessions interactive by encouraging a few of the staff to choose a beer and "present" it to the rest of group in much the same way they would to customers – saying why they like the beer, explaining the particular style and where the beer is brewed. Hopefully, they can also discuss beer-related issues including stock rotation, customers' queries and the usual "housekeeping" problems that crop up in the course of work.

In this way, new staff members will be inducted into an enthusiastic beer culture and staff effectively train themselves. But you can also call on the sales and marketing people from the breweries you deal with – they should be more than happy to come along and talk about their products and might even arrange a visit to their brewery for the staff.

POURING RITES

Pouring a glass of still table wine is relatively straightforward. Pouring a highly carbonated beverage like beer is another matter entirely, particularly as you need to create and retain a head of foam. And while there's plenty of lively debate on how to pour the perfect beer, there is usually more agreement about the desired result: a lovely glass of beer topped with an attractive collar of foam.

I like to tell people that we drink beer with our eyes first of all, before bringing our other sensory apparatus into play. A well-poured beer is a sight to behold and sends a frisson of anticipation through a thirsty drinker. And the head isn't just there for presentation, it's packed with flavour compounds and adds to the complex overall palate of the amber nectar (but more about that later).

Like most things in life, practice makes perfect, and whether you are pouring from a beer tap or bottle, the principles are basically the same. But, before you can pour a great-looking beer you absolutely, indisputably need ... a clean glass. We'll discuss glassware procedures in the following chapter, but rest assured that nothing kills the head on a beer quicker than traces of grease or washing-up detergent left on a glass. Once you've got a spotlessly clean glass, you're ready to start pouring.

It's important to realise that the head should be created in the base of the glass with the first part of the pour (this process is officially known as "crusting" and brewing boffins have been known to present papers on this very phenomenon at international conferences). The initial pour should produce some densely packed foam (packed with lots of tiny bubbles) which will settle out into a nice even head.

Sometimes you might see a novice bartender trying to "milk" the head by pouring the last bit from a greater height, but this inevitably produces a lumpy head full of large, uneven bubbles. If you don't create the basis for a good head in the first part of the pour, it's impossible to correct the mistake later on.

Most experts agree that you should hold the glass at an angle (about 45 degrees) and start pouring — whether from a beer tap or bottle — from slightly above the lip of the glass. For reasons of hygiene, the beer tap should never contact the beer glass: that telltale clink of metal on glass still makes my skin crawl whenever I hear it in a bar.

Some pundits say you should direct the initial pour into the bottom of the glass and then slow down the flow rate by tilting it and running the beer down the inside of the glass; others reckon you should direct the first stream of beer against the side of the tilted glass. I prefer the second method, but it does depend on variables such as the type of beer, and the size and shape of the glass.

There are also two schools of thought concerning whether you should fill the glass in one continuous pour or use the "two-part" pour. The latter is my preference when pouring from a beer tap and means filling the glass to about 75 per cent, putting it down on the draining rack to settle, and then topping it up without disturbing the head. This method is sometimes referred to as the "Sydney pour" in Melbourne and elsewhere, and is being more widely encouraged by premium beer marketers who see it as slightly theatrical and more appropriate to overall presentation of their higher-priced brands.

The flow rate of the beer is obviously crucially important to the head formation. Beer is poured from a fully open tap (otherwise you'll end

STEP ONE Holding the glass by the base, tilt it at 45 degrees and position the bottle above.

STEP TWO Start pouring the beer so it hits the side of the glass with enough vigour to create foam.

STEP THREE Adjust the beer flow, depending on how the head is forming in the glass.

STEP FOUR Start tilting the glass upright, slowing down the beer flow as you do so.

STEP FIVE For the perfect pour, the beer should reach the plimsoll line on the glass and – ideally – the head of foam should measure at least "two fingers".

up with a glass of foam) and the flow rate depends on the gas pressure set in the cellar. Some publicans have been known to prefer slower flow rates so they can actually pour beer quicker in the long run (less time waiting for foam to settle).

This was particularly the case with draught Guinness which, ideally, needs about seven minutes to pour and settle the perfect pint. That was deemed by some impatient publicans to be too long for a customer to wait. While it is possible to pour Guinness faster by tinkering with the gas pressure, it usually means that lovely collar of beige-coloured foam won't last all the way down the glass, as it should.

When pouring from a bottle, you are effectively controlling the speed

> ... we drink beer with our eyes first of all, before bringing our other sensory apparatus into play.

of the pour. If you are too timid in pouring, you simply won't create enough foam in the base of the glass; too vigorous and you'll end up with more foam than beer (a friend of mine calls these disasters "Indian beers" – they've got a head and a turban). With a bit of practice, you'll soon discover that the art of beer pouring is reasonably forgiving.

It's definitely a lot easier to demonstrate pouring techniques (or show them through a series of photographs) than it is to write about them. I certainly had plenty of practice, both working in the hospitality industry and at home, before I ever had to find a way of describing the activity in words. But as it works in practice, let's see if it works in theory!

THE PERFECT HEAD

Anyone who has visited Europe knows that a generous "two fingers" of foam is considered the norm for serving lagers over there. (The depth of the head should be at least the width of two fingers held together.) In an Australian public bar, such presentation would probably see the drinker reject the beer and mutter something like "the tide's a bit low". But things are slowly changing.

Some beer companies – like Matilda Bay Brewing – provide specially badged glasses marked with a plimsoll line that clearly shows how large the head should be poured. And their iconic Redback brand is poured with a particularly big head, as befits a Bavarian-style wheat beer (in

Munich, the local weizen beer comes in huge, vase-like glasses, topped with towering heads of foam).

Redback was probably the first Australian beer to be poured with an "oversized" head, back in the late 1980s. With a slice of lemon usually thrown in as well, the overall package really broke the mould of what most Aussies expected a beer to look and taste like. No wonder it became the darling of the so-called "boutique beer revolution".

Order a pilsener in Germany and you may wait up to 10 minutes while it is poured and settled in several stages, before it is finally delivered with a blooming head of foam rising above the rim of the glass and a natty, paper apron around the stem to collect drips. This is beer poured and presented with true reverence.

A pint of Guinness in Ireland is given a similar treatment and the barman will often slice the head flat with a plastic or metal "foam cutter" before the final top-up. Watching the tumbling and settling effect of a Guinness is a spectator sport of sorts and a minor masterpiece of beer theatre.

> No one beats the Belgians when it comes to the theatre of beer presentation.

But no one beats the Belgians when it comes to the theatre of beer presentation. Thankfully, we now have a string of Belgian beer cafes in this country where you can witness the intricate pouring procedure. Individual glasses of various shapes and sizes are first inverted and chill-rinsed over a jet of ice-cold water, then filled from a generous height, before the foam is sliced off with a flat metal foam cutter. Finally the glass is dunked into a sinkful of water – to rinse off any sticky traces of beer – and presented to the drinker on its own individually badged beer coaster.

Many of the potent Belgian bottled ales are served in stemmed goblets or balloon-type glasses and the lively bottle-fermentation means they have to be poured with great care. At the Moorgat brewery, on the outskirts of Antwerp, a marketing chap once timidly poured a glass of Duvel to show me the generously fluffy, white head on this legendary strong golden ale. Later, at a nearby restaurant, he was momentarily appalled when our flashy waiter poured two bottles of Duvel simultaneously (grasped in one hand) – with an impressive flourish – into a pair of balloon glasses held in the other. It was quite a performance and somehow he managed to deliver the perfect "three fingers" of foam (much to the marketing guy's relief).

When it comes to beer pouring and presentation, the annual Australian Draught Master Competition represents the equivalent of the Olympics for local hospitality staff. The event is sponsored by Stella Artois and began as an in-house competition among staff at the various Belgian beer cafes, but in recent years has been opened up to outside outlets that have Belgian beers on tap.

"The competition is usually decided on personality," says judge Robert Briers, who works as a consultant for Belgian brewing giant InBev in Australia. Entrants are scored out of a possible 250 points and must serve a table of four judges as if they were customers. They have seven minutes to welcome the "customers", tell them about the beers, take orders and then pour and present beers in the recommended manner.

While the beer order is always the same — two Stella Artois, one Hoegaarden and a Leffe Brune (poured from a bottle) — competitors have to remember who ordered what. They are closely scrutinised by the judging panel as they go through the prescribed tap pouring routine. "They must hold the glass at a 45-degree angle, then slowly straighten it, making sure the beer tap doesn't touch the glass or beer," Briers says.

The bottled beer must be poured in one continuous flow, with about one-fifth of the beer left in the bottle. "This is standard for all Belgian bottled beers," Briers says, because many have yeast deposits from secondary fermentation and it allows the customer the choice of drinking the yeasty remnants or not. Entrants are penalised one point for every five seconds they exceed the seven-minute limit and can also lose points for things like mispronouncing beer brands.

Obviously, nerves can play a big part in the performance, especially as state winners go on to compete for the national title, and the overall Australian Draught Master Competition winner later flies to Belgium for a shot at the international title. This is serious competitive behaviour, reflecting the reverence that the Belgians have for their national drink — and it's obviously about a lot more than simply pouring beer, with product knowledge, personality and table service all coming into play.

TABLE SERVICE

If an establishment offers table service, what is the correct etiquette for serving bottled beer? Should it be poured at the bar — just as with tap beer? Should it be poured at the table in front of the customer? Or should you simply serve the glass and opened bottle to the customer and let them pour their own?

The answer is that it really depends on the individual outlet, though my preference would be to treat bottled beer the same as wine and pour it at the table or, better still, give the customers the option of having it poured for them. An alternative is to half-fill the glass with a generous head and let the punter complete their own "second pour".

Many restaurants have separate waiting and bar staff, so that beer is poured at the bar (by a bartender) and then brought to the customer by the waiter or waitress. If wine is offered by the glass then it is also usually poured at the bar, whereas a bottle of wine will be opened and poured at the table. I reckon beer deserves to be treated the same way, especially as you are inevitably paying a hefty premium for it.

One of my pet hates is ordering a relatively expensive imported beer in a restaurant and then being brought a full glass without any sign of the bottle. It should be common courtesy to present the bottle in any case – to confirm the correct order, if nothing else – but more especially with imported beers, where freshness could be an issue.

POURING & SERVICE – DOs & DON'Ts

DO
- use a clean glass
- pour with enough vigour to create foam in the bottom of the glass
- tilt the glass to regulate the flow
- use the two-part pouring technique

Table service:
- bring the bottle and glass to the table
- offer to pour the beer for your customer

DON'T
- use dirty glassware
- let the beer tap or bottle contact the glass
- try to build a head by "milking" the last part of the pour

Table service:
- pour bottled beer behind the bar
- bring a full glass to the table without the bottle

GLASSWARE CARE

"Some bloke told me you should never wash your beer glass in detergent," said a customer when I was managing a Sydney homebrew shop some years ago. We were troubleshooting a problem he was having with his homebrew head collapsing in the glass as soon as it was poured. I asked him to bring a bottle into the shop, poured it into a clean glass and – hey presto – a beautiful, thick collar of foam stayed on top of the beer.

This customer had been religiously washing his beer glass in warm water only, because he'd been told that detergent will kill the head on your beer. The bloke who told him was half-right but, trouble is, without using detergent in the first place you can never completely remove traces of hop oil and other grease which, over time, will ruin your head retention.

The secret is to wash glasses in hot water and detergent, then thoroughly rinse off the detergent with more hot water and, finally, hand-dry them with a clean tea towel. My friend followed the advice and never had any problems with collapsing heads again.

I follow the same routine at home but the principles are the same for bars and restaurants, even if you are using an automatic dishwasher. The water has to be hot, you need the right amount of detergent to get glasses clean, plus an effective rinse cycle to leave them sparkling.

While automatic dishwashers are great time-savers, they don't necessarily do a perfect job. One pub I worked in would get the bar staff to wash every glass by hand on a weekly basis. That meant manually cleaning the inside of each glass with a brush arrangement set up in a bucket of warm, soapy water and then putting them through the rinse cycle in the dishwasher. It ensured that the glasses were spotlessly clean and it's a practice that I would encourage every outlet to follow.

The real enemies for beer glasses are things like lipstick, lip balm and grease from fried food, chips and peanuts, all of which will kill a head faster than Dirty Harry. A new, automatic dishwasher operating at peak efficiency will handle most things but there's really no replacement for good old elbow grease.

Years ago, I visited the Hopduvel cafe in Ghent which specialised in a mind-blowing selection of Belgian beers, each served with its individual glass. At the end of the night, every dirty glass was washed and rinsed by hand, and then the staff would hand-dry the lot with tea towels. It was a lengthy, tedious process – although one usually done with an end-of-shift beer close at hand – but it showed clearly the cafe's commitment to faultless beer presentation.

Hand-drying with tea towels is probably impractical for most bars and restaurants, but it is the only method of guaranteeing sparkling, streak-free glassware.

We now seem to live in the age of the "schmiddy", as many bars are getting away from the standard middy, pot or schooner glasses of old, and opting for a single, smart-looking glass. Anything that improves the visual appearance of the amber nectar is great, but I have seen some thin, tapered glasses that look elegant but are obviously impractical – they are too easy to knock over and less than dishwasher-friendly.

Increasingly, premium beer suppliers are now offering individually shaped and badged glassware in which to serve their products. This is the proverbial win-win situation for bar operators as it keeps their glassware costs down, while reinforcing brand awareness for the beer marketers.

Chilling beer glasses in fridges is still popular in the hotter parts of this country, but it's really not necessary if your cellar is functioning properly and the beer is being dispensed at the right temperature. Besides, it takes up valuable shelf space that could be used to display a wider range of beer.

In you're going to invest in premium glassware for a bar, then make sure it's appropriate to the beers that you pour. Specialised lager and pilsener glasses are usually taller, thinner and stemmed, while ales and stout can be served in chunky glasses, mugs or straight-sided pint glasses.

Many bars try to model themselves on English or Irish pubs and hang mugs up on hooks around the bar. It looks good and they're usually easier to reach than from a tray under the bar, but please make sure they are not anywhere near the smokers' zone!

GLASSWARE CARE – DOs & DON'Ts

DO

- use hot water and detergent, then rinse
- in busy bars, manually clean all glassware once a week
- use glasses that are appropriate to beer styles

DON'T

- wash glasses without detergent
- hang glasses from hooks near smoking areas
- use inappropriate, impractical glassware

STORING BEER

The Germans have a saying that goes along the lines: "You should only drink beer within sight of the brewery." That basically means drinking local beer because then you know it must be fresh, and in a country with 1000-odd breweries the logic is sound. And, it's certainly true that when it comes to beer, fresh is best. Most beer is in peak condition the day it leaves the brewery's front gate. Correctly stored, it will deteriorate only slowly over several months, but the greatest enemies to beer's freshness are heat and UV light.

The cool-room is the best place to store beer but, failing that, a cool, darkened area is the next best thing. Just like wine, beer prefers a constant, cooler temperature rather than being in some non-insulated area that suffers from temperature fluctuations. At home, the refrigerator is fine, but some bar fridge lighting (particularly the fluorescent variety) can cause beer to become "light-struck" over time.

Sommeliers are usually in charge of ordering and storing wine and our imagined beer sommelier would have a similar task. All beer should now display a "best by" date (some also list the manufacturing date) and a diligent sommelier would check these details on delivery. With imported beers, these dates are even more crucial as they are obviously going to be considerably older than any local products.

An importer once sent me a carton of beer that he was bringing in from a rather exotic corner of the world. He had previously phoned and told me, breathlessly, that several people (including his wife) thought it was the best beer they had ever tried and he wanted me to write about it. A few days later, he emailed to inquire how I had found the beer.

"Well," I replied, "it may have been a perfectly drinkable beer when fresh, but the sample you sent me was 18 months past its best-by date – it was a corpse of a beer!" In fact, the beer – which was a filtered lager – was so old it was hazy, full of tiny "floaties" and decidedly "winey". These are all telltale signs of age deterioration in a beer, but I didn't waste it: I used it to bait the snail and slug traps in the veggie garden for several months. I'd like to think those slimy critters met a happy end, sozzled on stale beer from the other side of the globe!

> The greatest enemies to beer's freshness are heat and UV light.

This was an extreme case but not entirely isolated, as I've been sent my share of tired and creaky imported lagers over the years. I now make a point of checking dates on labels, which give a pretty good indication of how fresh the contents will be.

Stock rotation is obviously important and our beer sommelier would make sure fridges are stocked from the back – if you keep replacing beer on the front of shelves, the older stock will be pushed further back in the fridge. Sooner or later – probably on a busy night – someone is going to be served some really old product.

A beer sommelier would also keep a close eye on stock turnover, watching out, in particular, for any slow-moving lines. Creating a discounted "beer of the week" or similar promotion is a good way to move beers that haven't proved so popular with customers. In the end, you can't afford to carry "passengers" on your beer-list.

Occasionally you see bars or bottleshops advertising "more than 100 different imported beers" but – while it's a nifty gimmick – it's virtually impossible to turnover fresh stock on every one of those brands. A well-constructed beer-list needs variety and breadth, rather than the scatter-gun, more-is-better approach.

Most pubs and bars get their keg beers delivered weekly, so stock rotation should be fairly straightforward. Kegs obviously aren't subject to UV light but heat can still affect their quality. Years ago, a mate and I adjourned to a Balmain pub for lunch on a baking-hot summer's day, only to find some newly delivered kegs sitting outside in the sun. Out of curiosity (or stupidity), we touched them and – Whoaaa! – nearly burnt our fingers because they had been sitting there for several hours.

A keg is just a big beer can and there's no excuse for allowing the contents of either to heat up in this way. Maybe the cellarman was sick or something, but kegs should be delivered directly to the cellar and stored appropriately.

EXCEPTIONS

While the vast majority of beer should be consumed as fresh as possible, there are some notable exceptions to the rule. Bottle-fermented beers – especially higher-alcohol ones like Belgian ales and barley wines – tend to hold condition longer in the cellar (though the same rules for correct storage apply).

Among them are a handful of strong specialty brews (Chimay Grande Réserve, Coopers Vintage Ale, Thomas Hardy's Ale, Unibroue Fringante, to name a few) which are vintage-dated and sometimes carry a best-by date of up to five years from the time of bottling. Whether these beers actually improve with age is debatable, but they certainly develop some unusual complexity over time.

In Belgium, I have sampled a 10-year-old bottle of Chimay Grande Réserve and a 20-year-old Orval. Both were still astonishingly drinkable for such senior citizens but were noticeably "madeirised" and slightly winey. I've also conducted a Chimay vertical tasting which showed a mellowing of flavour notes over the years and some serious deterioration of the corks (in a couple of cases).

If you really want to age some of these cork-stoppered rarities, then I recommend laying down the bottles on their side on a wine rack to keep the corks moist. Having said that, there is another school of thought among serious online beer geeks that such beer should be stored vertically. Take your pick and let me know the results (better still, invite me to sample the difference sometime).

Be aware, also, that cork taint can affect these beers. Trichloroanisole (TCA) is said to affect about five per cent of all wine corks, so there's no reason to think corked beers will be immune. If customers complain of cork taint or an oxidised (or otherwise spoilt) beer then they should receive similar treatment as for wine: open a fresh bottle to compare and return any "suspect" products to the distributor (who should replace such items with fresh stock).

BEER STORAGE – DOs & DON'Ts

DO
- store bottled beer in a cool room or cool area
- check best-by dates on imported beer
- rotate stock in fridges

DON'T
- expose beer to excessive heat or UV light
- carry too many "passengers" (slow-moving lines) on your beer-list
- stock fridges by replacing missing stock from the front of shelves

DESIGNING A BALANCED BEER-LIST

How much thought goes into creating the average beer list? Not very much when you see four or five light beers and the usual, ho-hum range of imported lagers, or a list that is obviously largely drawn from the brand portfolio of either of our two major brewing companies.

Such lists are driven by the producers and distributors, rather than being designed with the individual outlet or consumer in mind. And I can't tell you how many times I've seen inspired and creative restaurant wine-lists backed up with a token, mindless offering of beers.

A balanced beer-list should ideally cover several style bases while offering sufficient variety (with a scattering of genuinely interesting brews), but it has to be appropriate for the venue and, above all, commercially viable. There's little point in offering a catalogue of world classics if your clientele comprises mainly die-hard Crownie and VB drinkers.

While I personally believe that life is too short to drink light beer, I acknowledge that there is a place for such products and, indeed, some states legally require licensed outlets to offer at least one low-alcohol beer. The law, as they say, is an ass – why aren't they also required to offer low-alcohol versions of wine and spirits, for instance? But let's leave that argument for another day.

Most people drink light beer under sufferance – usually, they are driving or otherwise want to moderate their intake of alcohol. They may have a favoured light beer brand but it is unlikely to be their favourite brand of beer, overall – it is their "default" brand under certain circumstances. These consumers will probably order light beer whatever the choice is and, really, two different brands is probably more than enough for most outlets.

Many restaurant beer-lists are top-heavy with lagers – consisting of several light beers, local premium lagers and a handful of imported lagers, with perhaps a token Guinness or Coopers cloudy ale thrown in. This is inexcusably feeble, especially given the variety of beer styles now being brewed in Australia, all of which can be readily matched with food (more about that shortly).

I've seen restaurant lists that feature what I call "the usual suspects" – Crown Lager, Hahn Premium Lager, Cascade Premium Lager, James Boag Premium Lager, Heineken, Stella Artois, Corona and Beck's – all offered by the bottle – and little else besides. Trouble is, these are all essentially variations on a single beer theme – the premium or export lager. It is like offering eight different chardonnays and nothing else.

> Many restaurant beer lists are top-heavy with lagers ... this is inexcusably feeble, especially given the variety of beer styles now being brewed in Australia.

I suspect this sort of mindless selection is a hangover from a bygone era, when blokes had a few beers before lunch, drank wine with their meal and then ended up with several "cleansing ales" afterwards (which, more than likely, were actually lagers). Anyway, you could offer half the number of these brands and still cater for most tastes while slotting in a few local craft beers or varied brews.

Pubs and bars, at least, seem to give more thought to beer selection. Ideally there should be a reasonable spread with mainstream brands complemented by a fair range of domestic premiums, imports and some representatives from the local craft sector.

Tap beer is the bread and butter of most pubs, and getting it right is a neat balancing act. But, really, any beer-list should be seen as a work in progress with, perhaps, a couple of taps rotating "guest beers". Your customers will soon tell you whether one of these newer brews is selling enough volume to warrant a permanent tap space.

I can't see the point in duplicating the same brand on tap and in the bottle. Given the choice, most punters would prefer their favourite beer from the tap (it should be fresher and better value). Also, why take up valuable space on fridge shelves that could be catering for the "repertoire" drinker who's looking for something a little different.

MY WISH LIST

TAP BEERS

The range of tap beers you can offer really depends on a reasonable turnover of the slower-moving lines. Outside mainstream beers, my tap beer wish list would include at least one from each of the following:

Imported Lagers Heineken, Stella Artois, Beck's

Domestic Premium Lagers Hahn Premium, Cascade Premium, Bluetongue Premium Lager

Craft Lagers James Squire Pilsener, Matilda Bay Bohemian Pilsner, Gage Roads Pure Malt Lager

Craft Ales Little Creatures Pale Ale, James Squire Amber Ale, Coopers Sparkling Ale, Mountain Goat Hightail Ale

Summer Seasonals James Squire Golden Ale, Redback

Winter Seasonals James Squire Porter, Coopers Extra Stout, Holgate Winter Ale

Ideally, there would also be a rotating "guest" tap where various craft brews could be trialled.

BOTTLED BEERS

Any beer-list should be a work in progress, with slow-moving lines dropped and a regular turnover of seasonal or "out-there" beers. Finding an ideal balance will always be tricky, but here's a selection of 24 beers as a possible line-up for an upmarket bar:

Lagers James Boag Premium Light, James Boag Premium Lager, Crown Lager, Cascade Premium Lager, Bluetongue Premium Lager, Gage Roads Pure Malt Lager

Pilseners James Squire Original Pilsener, Matilda Bay Bohemian Pilsner, Trumer Pils

Darker Lagers Matilda Bay Rooftop Red Lager, James Squire Amber Ale

Wheat Beers Redback, Hoegaarden Wit

Ales Coopers Pale Ale, Coopers Sparkling Ale, Little Creatures Pale Ale, Holgate Pale Ale, Mountain Goat Hightale Ale
Porters/Dark Ales Monteiths Black Ale, James Squire Porter
Stout Coopers Extra Stout, Old Southwark Stout
Strong Ales Chimay Blue, Duvel

DEVELOPING A BEER PALATE

As I've said earlier, most Australian beer consumers drink labels, in effect. By that, I mean they choose particular brands because of various perceptions related to status, lifestyle, loyalty and – occasionally – flavour. Beer marketing people call these consumers "badge drinkers" and it implies that brand choice is some sort of reflection of their personality and aspirations.

Brand loyalty is a fickle beast and modern beer advertising generally relies on humour to somehow make the consumer feel good about their choice of product. Most Aussie beer drinkers have strong opinions about which brands are better; unfortunately, it often has little to do with flavour.

"I love my Crownie but I can't stand that Foster's muck," is the sort of statement I've heard countless times over the years. Trouble is, such opinions are based on extremely shaky ground when put to the taste test.

I reckon about half of such opinionated drinkers would choose Foster's Lager over Crown Lager in a blind taste test. If you don't believe me, try it out for yourself. The flavour profile (or palate) of these beers is so similar that most drinkers would struggle to tell them apart.

How is it, then, that one brand sells in excess of four million cases a year, while the other has almost dropped off the radar? Like I said: most people drink beer labels, not beer flavour, and their preferences are usually based on perceptions rather than reality.

A blind beer tasting is the ultimate leveller and can be an extremely humbling experience for certain loud-mouthed drinkers. But it's also the best way for an aspiring beer sommelier to develop a beer palate and to appreciate flavour components in individual beers.

I don't believe anyone is born with a natural beer palate but some people are certainly more naturally gifted in detecting flavour nuances. Your palate is a bit like a muscle and, with regular exercise and the right training regime, it's possible for anyone to develop a discerning beer palate.

And, hey, there's no reason why you shouldn't have a bit of fun along the way. Why not organise an informal beer tasting with a few of your mates and get everyone to bring a bottle wrapped in a brown paper bag (or otherwise suitably masked). Encourage them to try to describe the beer's appearance, aroma and flavour, and whether they like it or not (it works best if you write down your comments so they are "locked in" before the beer's identity is revealed).

Not only are they fun, these "brown paper bag" sessions usually push everyone to actually think about flavour components and beer styles. If you hold them on a weekly basis, you will soon cultivate budding beer palates.

Trying to find the appropriate words to describe beer aromas and flavour can be a real challenge in the beginning, and it often depends on an individual's memory bank of smells and tastes. Food and wine lovers

> Most people drink beer labels, not beer flavour, and their preferences are usually based on perceptions rather than reality.

will find it easier to draw on comparative flavours but we all perceive such elements in slightly different ways.

A few years ago I was conducting a blind tasting of ales for a magazine when we encountered a particularly fruity, bottle-fermented sample. "Ah – I can smell apricots," I said. "Peaches!" another taster pronounced. "I get nectarines," said another. "I don't eat fruit!" declared a fourth taster (who was deadly serious). Needless to say, we cracked up with laughter but it did illustrate an important point: if you don't taste a wide range of food and drink, how are you going to describe various flavour notes?

Larger breweries usually conduct weekly tasting sessions of their products to ensure consistency and to detect any possible flavour faults. Mainstream brewers talk about developing a "cellar palate" which is highly attuned to detect off-flavours or slight differences in flavour profiles. But that is beer tasting of a highly technical nature, and we're more interested in encouraging budding beer sommeliers to taste a wide variety of beer styles and flavours.

However, there is one blind beer tasting technique employed by mainstream brewers called the "triangular test", which is particularly useful for untrained palates. It involves presenting two different beers spread over three samples, in other words, two of the three samples are the same beer. The challenge for the taster is to detect the matched pair from the odd one out.

Obviously, it works best with similar style beers – mainstream lagers, premium lagers or suchlike. Some breweries use dark-coloured glasses and special lighting so that the beer's colour or appearance is indistinguishable. At home, you can simply choose beers whose appearance is difficult to tell apart.

Tasting a range (or flight) of beers of a similar style is the best way to detect flavour nuances and "house styles" within fairly tight parameters. By using the table featured later in this chapter, you can design your tasting session around an individual style – domestic premium lagers, pilseners, imported lagers, wheat beers, pale ales, stouts and porters, and so on.

I recommend these "style" sessions for more advanced tasters who have already developed a descriptive vocabulary and a reasonably discerning palate. Once you've found a few reliable fellow-tasters who've been on the educational flavour journey, you'll find these sessions particularly valuable. And if you're comfortable that everyone's on a similar level, then there's really no need to mask the labels.

For beginners, it's worth staging one session that covers a wide range of different styles. A flight that includes a mainstream lager (Victoria Bitter), a premium lager (James Boag's Premium Lager), a pilsener (Matilda Bay Bohemian Pilsner), a bottle-fermented ale (Mountain Goat Hightail Ale), an aromatic pale ale (Little Creatures Pale Ale), a spicy wheat beer (Hoegaarden Wit) and a full-bodied stout (Coopers Extra Stout), would be a good starting point.

AN ORGANOLEPTIC EXPERIENCE

How, exactly, should you taste beer and what are you supposed to be looking for? Anyone who's been to an organised wine tasting will be familiar with the sniff, swirl and slurp routine, and it's basically the same approach for beer.

Some brewers describe a beer tasting as an "organoleptic experience", which sounds like a rather grandiose exercise but simply means that we are using our "organs of sense" to experience the various characteristics of a beer.

I sometimes tell people that beer tasting is a "sensual experience" and that we should use all five senses to extract maximum enjoyment from the amber nectar. Let's see how each sense relates to beer and how we use it during a tasting session.

EYES

Figuratively speaking – and before anything else comes into play – we drink beer with our eyes. We admire the colour and note the clarity (or otherwise), carbonation and, not least, head formation, which really sets beer apart from other alcoholic beverages.

Professional beer tasters call this the beer's "appearance" and award marks according to the individual characteristics I've outlined. So let's look at them one by one.

Colour

Beer comes in a wide spectrum of colours ranging from the palest lemon, through gold, amber, reddish-brown and black. The colour of a beer usually provides a strong clue to its possible style and flavour, and results from the types of grain used (except in rare cases where coloured brewing sugars or – shock, horror! – caramel colouring agents have been used).

Clarity

The vast majority of beer is filtered before packaging to attain "star bright" clarity. With pale golden lagers, in particular, pristine clarity is vital and mainstream brewers are obsessed with preventing things like "chill haze" which can occur when certain proteins in beer are chilled. In such cases, any sign of haze would be marked down as a fault.

But in certain beer styles – notably, hefeweizen (cloudy wheat beer) and bottle-fermented ale (like Coopers Sparkling Ale) – haziness is deliberate and should not be penalised by beer judges. In these cases, the beer has usually been dosed with live yeast to promote a secondary fermentation in the bottle or keg.

Here, yeastiness is a desirable characteristic, whereas in lagers, every effort has been made to remove any traces of yeast.

Carbonation

Apart from some extremely rare exceptions (Unibroue Quelque Chose is one that springs to mind), all beer should be carbonated. And while those carbon dioxide bubbles create a lovely head of foam on your glass, they also concentrate certain flavour compounds (dip your finger in foam and taste just how bitter it is), and are "felt" in the mouthfeel.

The level of carbonation can vary from relatively soft (English real ales poured from the cask), to well-carbonated (most Australian mainstream lagers), through to "lively" or highly carbonated (e.g. Bavarian hefeweizen, Chimay, Leffe, Deus, Duvel and a whole host of Belgian strong ales). These varying carbonation levels are entirely appropriate to each particular style of beer.

The size of the bubbles moving upwards in the glass can also indicate something about the maturation time the beer has undergone. In a German lager or Czech pilsener, you might notice a trail of tiny, slow-moving bubbles that results from a lengthy period of maturation (or lagering, as the Germans call it).

The size of the bubble can also affect head formation and we can talk about a "tightly packed" or "densely formed" collar of foam on a beer. Naturally carbonated and bottle-fermented beers normally have a prominent "rocky" (or uneven) head, which I've sometimes heard described as a "cauliflower" head.

By tilting the partially filled glass from side to side, you can observe the cling or lacing of bubbles − produced by the foam against the side of the glass. Of course, all these visual aspects relating to the head rely on scrupulously clean glasses (and we presume everyone has fully digested the chapter on glassware care before staging any beer tastings!).

The beer foam that forms inside the glass is called "Brussels lace" and is another sign of a well-made beer (and a clean glass). When you finish a full glass of beer (in a bar, rather than in a judging session) − you should be able to see a series of foam rings down the side of the glass, recording each satisfying mouthful.

> beer tasting is a sensual experience ... we should use all five senses to extract maximum enjoyment from the amber nectar.

NOSE

Sniffing a glass of beer in a public bar is not necessarily the best way to endear yourself to the publican, but it is part of the appreciation process for the aspiring beer judge. Obviously, it works better with a partly filled glass, so you can swirl the beer (to release aromatic notes) and actually stick your nose into the glass.

The so-called "nose" of beer is rather shy, especially compared to that of wine or whisky. Because it is normally served chilled and has a relatively modest alcohol level, beer has relatively few volatile aromatics compared to those other, stronger beverages.

Training your bugle to pick up delicate and fleeting notes will probably be the greatest challenge to the novice beer taster. But – rest assured – in time and with plenty of practice, you will develop a discerning nose for beer.

Allowing your beer sample to warm up slightly will help open up its aromatic secrets, but many beers smell malty and little else besides. We beer writers often describe the nose on lagers as being "clean", meaning there are no complexities or discernible "off-flavours".

Ingredients

The nose on some beers will show aromatic or "floral" hoppiness, while others will offer fruity notes which are usually created by various yeasty esters or, perhaps, roasty or coffee-like notes (from roasted malted barley). When you realise that a beer's palate is simply a product of the main ingredients – hops, grain and yeast – at least you know what sort of aroma and flavour notes to look for.

Familiarising yourself with beer's raw ingredients is an important step in the appreciation process. Homebrewers who "customise" their cans of concentrate with a few extra hops or some coloured grains are using these ingredients much as a home cook might jazz up a packaged meal with some onion, chilli or herbs. Importantly, they are learning how these different elements contribute various flavours to the finished beer.

Our potential beer sommeliers don't have to take up homebrewing (though it would certainly help with their beer appreciation) but they should try to get up close and personal with beer's raw ingredients. Most brewery tours provide samples of hops and grains for you to sniff and taste, otherwise you should visit your local homebrew shop where they will happily sell you something appropriate.

Perhaps you can stage an "ingredients sampling" as part of one of your regular beer tasting sessions. If you tell the homebrew shop what you're doing, they might be able to package up small sample bags of different hops and grains.

A single hop flower or pellet can be crushed between your palms and gently sniffed. Depending on the variety, you'll probably detect spicy, resinous, floral or citrussy notes. Hops are the basic seasoning in beer and the oily resins have been used to bitter beer for centuries; this bitterness counterpoints the sweetness of the malt sugars and is present – to some degree – in all beers.

However – used at different stages of the brewing process – hops can also contribute delicate aromas and flavours which all add to the complexity of the beer. Notably aromatic local brews include Little

ALES
WARMER FERMENTATION PRODUCES FRUITY AND COMPLEX FLAVOURS

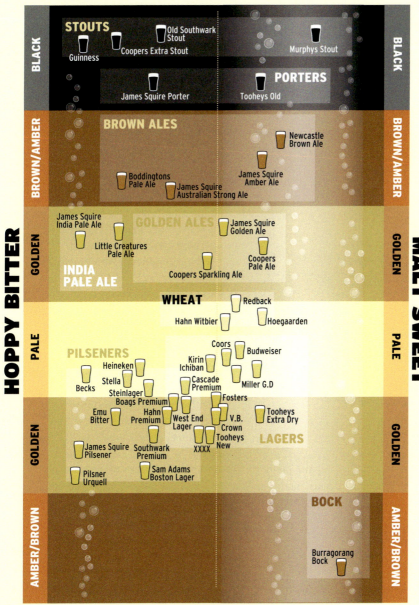

HOPPY BITTER

MALT SWEET

BLACK | BROWN/AMBER | GOLDEN | PALE | GOLDEN | AMBER/BROWN

STOUTS
Guinness
Coopers Extra Stout
Old Southwark Stout
Murphys Stout

PORTERS
James Squire Porter
Tooheys Old

BROWN ALES
Boddingtons Pale Ale
James Squire Australian Strong Ale
James Squire Amber Ale
Newcastle Brown Ale

GOLDEN ALES
James Squire India Pale Ale
Little Creatures Pale Ale
Coopers Sparkling Ale
James Squire Golden Ale
Coopers Pale Ale

INDIA PALE ALE

WHEAT
Hahn Witbier
Redback
Hoegaarden

PILSENERS
Becks
Heineken
Stella
Steinlager
Boags Premium
Emu Bitter
Hahn Premium
James Squire Pilsener
Southwark Premium
Pilsner Urquell
Sam Adams Boston Lager

Kirin Ichiban
Cascade Premium
West End Lager
XXXX
Coors
Budweiser
Miller G.D
Fosters
V.B.
Crown
Tooheys New
Tooheys Extra Dry

LAGERS

BOCK
Burragorang Bock

COOLER FERMENTATION PRODUCES A DRIER FINISH
LAGERS

Creatures Pale Ale and James Squire Original Pilsener, and this pair is a good starting point to try to identify hop aromas.

Another way to familiarise yourself with different hop flavours is to prepare hop teas – put half a dozen hop pellets or flowers into a large mug and half-fill with boiling water. Allow the hops to steep for several minutes and then nose them – using several different hop varieties is a great way to discern their individual characteristics.

Pale malted barley is the heart and soul of all beer and contributes the fermentable sugars that yeast turns into alcohol and carbon dioxide. A beer made entirely from pale malted barley will be pale golden in colour; adding relatively small amounts of coloured or "specialty" malts will darken the final beer and contribute significantly different flavours and aromas.

Crystal malt has a nutty, biscuit-like character and, typically, is used in amber ales and red lagers (James Squire Amber Ale, Newcastle Brown Ale, Matilda Bay Rooftop Red Lager). Chocolate malt is so-called because of its colour but it can contribute chocolate-like notes and is often used in conjunction with roasted malt or roasted barley (as in James Squire Porter). Both these roasted grains look a bit like dark-roasted coffee beans and, not surprisingly, they provide espresso-like characters and darker colours to beers like Coopers Extra Stout and Guinness.

Wheat beers are often the palest of beers and are usually made from roughly 50 per cent malted wheat and malted barley. Wheat contributes a distinctly tart and refreshing note, and promotes a noticeably lively head.

> Our potential beer sommeliers don't have to take up homebrewing (though it would certainly help with their beer appreciation).

Yeast is basically the catalyst for the fermentation process but can also contribute its own particular character to beer. It's most noticeable in ales – especially bottle-fermented ones like Coopers Sparkling Ale or Mountain Goat Hightail Ale – where the fruity esters (produced by the yeast during fermentation) have aroma and flavour notes similar to certain fruits like apricots or peaches.

Wheat beers (like Schneider or Franziskaner Hefe-weissbier) feature some of the most upfront and complex yeast aromas to be found, full of fruity, spicy characters (clove, banana and bubblegum are commonly used descriptors).

Spoiled beer

If you can, get hold of some stale, oxidised or otherwise spoiled beer for one of your tasting sessions. Once you experience the unpleasant off-flavours, you'll begin to appreciate why "clean" is a desirable description, particularly with lagers.

Unfortunately, it's not too difficult to find an imported beer on a bottleshop shelf that has gone beyond its best-by date and – for the sake of our knowledge journey – it would be great to slip such a sample into one of your blind tasting sessions.

Stale beer will often pour with a weak head that rapidly disappears or shows varying sized foam bubbles, including telltale large ones (sometimes described as an "egg shell" effect). But the smell will be more alarming – damp paper (or cardboard), floury or winey notes usually mean the beer is stale and oxidised. Seriously old beer will appear hazy and may even contain tiny particles or "floaties".

Nosing a spoilt beer alongside a fresh one is the best way to identify the telltale signs of age. Once encountered, they should impinge on your flavour memory so that you can spot a stale beer with one sniff. For me, it was years spent reviewing hundreds of imported beers for a certain wine magazine that allowed me to sample more over-the-hill beer than most people would encounter in a single lifetime.

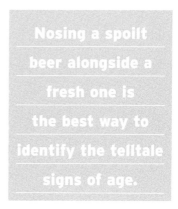

Nosing a spoilt beer alongside a fresh one is the best way to identify the telltale signs of age.

MOUTH (TASTE)

We've assessed the beer's appearance and nosed its delicate aromas, now is the time to analyse its taste. And while our tongues are covered with tiny tastebuds that pick up different types of flavour, it's important to realise that the nose is actually the principal organ of taste.

Try tasting beer with a blocked nose or heavy cold (or simply by closing your nostrils with finger and thumb) and you'll see what I mean. Without being able to use your nasal apparatus, all beer will simply taste cold, wet and fizzy.

Different areas of the tongue detect different basic flavours: sweetness on the tip of the tongue, saltiness and sourness at the sides, and bitterness at the back. In conjunction with our nasal receptors, then, we taste the beer in different stages as it rolls across the tongue and is swallowed. The initial "palate" may be sweet and malty, the middle palate may show various complexities and subtle flavour notes, while the "finish" will be bitter and, possibly, lingering.

To taste beer we simply take a mouthful (with some air), roll it around the mouth and then swallow. Some beer tasters actually spit but, really, bitterness can be best experienced by swallowing and, unlike wine, the aftertaste is important.

One or two mouthfuls is usually enough to evaluate the flavour profile and I also find that first impressions are the strongest (if you keep returning to earlier samples during a beer tasting, you inevitably end up more confused than ever).

"I've drunk plenty of beer but I've never had to think about it before," said a fellow taster during an organised session. It's true – we usually drink beer for refreshment and enjoyment and only a few of us take it seriously enough to try to put our impressions into words.

Building up a vocabulary of descriptive terms is part of the tasting experience, and the table of aroma and flavour descriptions below is a good starting point. I would encourage you to try to be as creative as possible, drawing on your own flavour memory but try to avoid the worst of wine's elitest descriptions such as "crushed autumn leaves mixed with ozone and tobacco".

MOUTHFEEL (TOUCH)

Holding beer on our tongue briefly and swirling it around the mouth before swallowing allows us to "feel" its texture or mouthfeel. A highly carbonated beer may feel spitzy or tingly, while some strong beers have a champagne-like mousse texture.

Mouthfeel is also related to "body" or what my wine colleagues might call "weight". Many mainstream beers are relatively thin-bodied (they are usually brewed with a portion of cane sugar and various adjuncts which add nothing to the beer's body), while full malt beers (made with 100 per cent malted barley) will feel reasonably full-bodied. And, in general, the stronger the beer, the fuller the body.

Common Beer Aroma/Flavour Descriptors

Spicy (cloves, pepper, yeasty)
Fruity (citrus, grapefruit, apricot, banana)
Grainy (grassy, nutty, honey, corn, caramel, toffee)
Roasty (coffee, chocolate, mocha, licorice)
Hoppy (floral, resinous, herbaceous, bitter)

Common faults

Winey, skunky, cooked vegetable, green apple,
sour, cheesy, papery, astringent, sulphur, medicinal

EARS

There is no category for sound on a beer judge's sheet. But we've already used our senses of sight, smell, taste and feel to analyse beer, so why not use our ears as well?

Because beer does have a sound – think of the *PZZZT* when you open a bottle or can, or the click of a beer tap and the gentle glug-glug-glug of beer being poured. These sounds are universal to all beers (no beer actually sounds better than another) and to a thirsty punter, they are music to one's ears.

The sound and sight of a beer being poured are part of the anticipation stage – you may even start salivating – and should never be overlooked. But don't worry, you'll never have to award a beer a score out of ten for its individual sound – just sit back and enjoy it.

MATCHING BEER WITH FOOD

Beer has tremendous versatility when it comes to matching it with food, and there is plenty of scope for listing specific beer suggestions on menus. Many outlets feature a wine recommendation (often by the glass) with different dishes, so why not list a suggested beer as well?

Occasionally I've spotted bar menus offering a special deal along the lines of "herbed lamb cutlets with a middy of amber ale" for an all-inclusive price. It's certainly sending the right message to the consumer: that this is a beer to enjoy with food, and might even attract some punters to try the beer for the first time.

> The right beer can reach heights of compatibility that wine simply can't achieve.

Beer is basically a more informal beverage than wine and is therefore well-matched with less formal fare like gourmet pizzas or beer-battered fish and chips. But it can just as easily be partnered with all manner of cuisine and – especially where chilli and spice or chocolate are ingredients – the right beer can reach heights of compatibility that wine simply can't achieve.

Choosing an appropriate style of beer to accompany a particular dish requires a mixture of common sense and imagination. While there is a fair degree of flexibility involved, a great beer mismatched with the wrong food flavours will still stand out like a tuxedo-clad gent at a wharfies' picnic.

Whenever he's hosting beer dinners around the country, Lion Nathan brewmaster Bill Taylor talks about the "three Cs" of matching the amber nectar with food, which stand for beer's ability to cleanse (or cut), complement or contrast.

CLEANSE

A well-chilled lager can cut through complex flavours – especially chilli-laced, highly spiced Asian or Mexican dishes, cooked cheese (as in pizzas), and oily, fried food – and effectively cleanse and refresh the palate. The carbonated nature of beer aids the cleansing process and even the blandest of lagers (like Corona and Kingfisher) deserve a place on the dining table to douse a fiery burrito or white-hot vindaloo. But more highly bittered beers like pilseners will also do the job, as the lingering bitterness refreshes the palate in readiness for the next mouthful of food.

A "grease-cutter" may not be the most elegant term but it describes neatly beer's ability to cut through the inherent oiliness of fried food. Add some saltiness, as in fish and chips, and a cold lager is hard to beat; the same goes for Thai fish cakes, samosas, salt and pepper calamari, or any other tasty fried delight.

Apparently the jury is still out as to whether any wine can cope with the mouth-coating, fatty nature of most cheese, and the same can probably be said for beer. There is just something about the cheesy texture coating one's palate that seems to neutralise and mute the subtle flavours of any beverage.

But, here again, beer's cleansing ability certainly makes a better fist than the fermented grape, and brown or amber ales go well with nutty cheeses like cheddar and gruyere. Salty cheeses like fetta or pecorino work well with pale lagers, while cooked cheese (as in things like pizza or Welsh rarebit) is another matter entirely and is supremely matchable with any cleansing beer.

COMPLEMENT

Choosing a beer to complement a dish is really a matter of picking a common flavour characteristic in both beverage and food. Obviously, lighter-flavoured beers belong with lighter flavoured food, so that premium lagers are well-matched with unadorned seafood like natural oysters, lightly cooked prawns or grilled fish.

A spicy beer like Hoegaarden Wit goes particularly well with a seafood risotto made with chopped, fresh coriander leaves (and you should use the beer instead of white wine in cooking the dish). Chicken and pork call for a slightly more flavoursome beer style like Vienna lager or an Oktoberfest beer. And think about how the caramelised flavours of grilled lamb cutlets or a chicken caesar salad (with bacon pieces) might be complemented by similar flavour notes in amber ale or a beer like Matilda Bay Rooftop Red Lager.

Moretti La Rossa is an Italian red lager that seems ready made for matching with pizza, with the beer echoing the flavour notes of the bready pizza base and cooked tomato topping. Gourmet pizzas with spicy ingredients like chorizo or Italian sausage might be partnered with Little Creatures Pale Ale, which has enough hoppy characters to complement the spicy meat.

The nutty notes in a beer like Newcastle Brown Ale can be matched with a crunchy summer salad featuring walnuts and fried bacon bits, while a spicy pale ale is just the ticket with something like a chilled Thai salad. German-style smoked beers are rare in Australia but Redoak Rauchbier would do wonders for smoked chicken or any dish featuring ham.

> Choosing a beer to complement a dish is really a matter of picking a common flavour characteristic in both beverage and food.

We've seen how a chilled lager will cleanse the palate when confronted with a lively curry, but some beers have enough bitterness and complexity to complement the piquant flavours of Asian cuisine. India pale ales – as the name suggests – make for a blissful match with the likes of a chicken vindaloo, with the higher alcohol and robust bitterness coping well with the spice and chilli hit.

Singha Lager from Thailand has a full palate and enough alcohol to balance the spicy complexity of many Thai dishes, while an acquaintance of mine swears by the Belgian Trappist ale Orval, as the only beer that can successfully complement a fiery seafood laksa.

Where beer has been used in the cooking process – as with beef carbonnade or stout and beef pie – then, quite obviously, that same beer should be drunk with the dish. One of my favourite Belgian meals is a dish of slow-cooked rabbit and prunes, which I've had variously made with Chimay Blue, Leffe Brune and Grimbergen Double; another is duck and sour cherries cooked in kriek. (No prizes for guessing which beer should be matched with these examples of cuisine de la biere.) A hearty winter meal of lamb shanks also calls for a robust dark ale.

The Bavarians love a mid-morning snack of weisswurst (a light-flavoured veal sausage) with a pale weisse beer, but will drink a dark lager with a more robustly flavoured sausage like bratwurst or kransky. The roasty flavours of Dogbolter or Löwenbräu Dunkel cope well with those robust fried meat characters (as well as the sweet, caramelised fried onions that go so well with all manner of wurst).

Stouts and other strong, dark brews really come into their own with rich desserts, particularly where chocolate or coffee flavourings feature. Try Old Southwark Stout with chocolate mud cake or Carbine Stout with a coffee-scented bavarois, or any number of Belgian specialty ales with a sweet-toothed confection – Gouden Carolus with pralines or Belgian truffles, Hoegaarden Forbidden Fruit with sabayon (made with the same spicy, dark ale) or Westmalle Double with sticky date pudding.

> A plate of natural oysters and a pint of creamy stout is a match made in beer gourmand's heaven.

Some spiced, strong dark ales such as Redoak Wee Heavy or Hoegaarden Forbidden Fruit can taste a bit like Christmas pudding in a glass, and can be successfully married with classic steamed puddings or a slice of fruit cake. Oatmeal stouts have a particularly silky character that lends itself to matching well with creamy concoctions like marsala or atholl brose.

Fruit beers are another natural partner for desserts. At the Jamieson Hotel in the Victorian high country, I once enjoyed a mini pavlova topped with chocolate sauce and fresh raspberries with a glass of Jamieson's Raspberry Ale.

Any of the Belgian fruit lambic beers – cherries, raspberries, blackcurrants and peaches are variously used – could be matched with sweets featuring the same fruit while the unusual apple-flavoured Unibroue Ephemere is just made for an apple pie or crumble. Hoegaarden Wit is flavoured with dried curacao peel which lends itself to an orange-tinged dessert match, while Bavarian hefeweizens show banana and clove characters that suggest sweets along the same lines (perhaps a spiced banana flambe).

CONTRAST

A plate of natural oysters and a pint of creamy stout is a match made in beer gourmand's heaven, and the combination works despite the obvious contrast in flavours. Somehow the burnt, roasty, bitter notes wrapped in that creamy texture suit the salty, succulent and sensuous oysters in the most marvellous manner.

"It was a brave man who ate the first oyster," someone once famously said, but it was a much smarter soul who first thought to wash them down with stout. Perhaps it happened in Ireland first, although Charles Dickens's novels feature plenty of Victorian gents hoovering up oysters and drinking mugs of porter. Some breweries have even tried to capture the best of both worlds by producing an oyster stout.

Porter and stout can also be matched with many other types of shellfish – mussels, clams, even crab and crayfish – with similar success. The peppery dryness of a well-bittered brew will effectively counterpoint the briny notes provided by a mixed seafood platter.

As covered earier in the Cleanse section, salty and fishy flavours are perhaps the best examples of successful contrasting combos with a crisp lager. The Indonesians have a snack called ikan bilis – a salty, crisp fried concoction of dried whitebait and peanuts – that is a fine match with a chilled Bintang or your favourite lager.

The crunchy texture of ikan bilis provides a further, tactile contrast and it's no surprise that many of the world's favourite beer snacks have a similar counterpoint to a mouthful of the amber nectar – potato crisps, peanuts, pretzels or sliced radishes dunked in salt. Similarly, the sour flavours of pickled onions, olives, gherkins and sauerkraut are a good foil for most lagers, wheat beers and pale ales.

Beer and cheese works best for me when both are strongly flavoured, so that a ripe blue or aged cheddar might be partnered with Chimay Grande Réserve, a barley wine or a strong, dark ale. Here, beer is employed much like a good port, which has enough depth of flavour and alcohol to cope with the full-on cheesy taste.

BEER DINNERS

As with wine, it's best to progress from light flavoured beers through to more complex, robust and high-alcohol styles, wherever possible. This can be a problem if you want to serve the classic stout and oysters pairing as an entree but, at one beer dinner I attended, they got around this hurdle neatly by serving a flute of Black Velvet (half stout, half sparkling wine).

Because beer is inherently more filling than wine, it makes sense to design a degustation menu encompassing several smaller courses matched with modest beer servings (175-200ml is probably sufficient). A variation is to offer two different beers with each course, either two examples of a similar style (for instance, a local and imported pilsener) or two distinctly different beer styles to illustrate the complement and contrast principles. I love the idea of the tasting boards on offer at the Redoak Boutique Beer Cafe in Sydney, where four tapas-inspired servings are matched with sample-sized glasses of their house brews.

The range of seafood, meat, vegetarian and sweets boards are ever-changing but always feature innovative combinations like seafood chowder and hefeweizen, lamb tongue and bock, quail egg and pale ale, poached pineapple and chocolate stout.

BEERS THAT LOVE FOOD

Brown and Amber Ales chicken, nutty salads, lightly grilled red meat, apple pie
Dark Lagers bratwurst, gourmet sausages, pastrami
Pilseners and Premium Lagers fish, natural oysters, fried snacks, salty cheeses (such as fetta)
English Pale Ales and Sparkling Ales lamb, beef
Fruit-based Beers fruit dessert
Red Ales and Red Lagers chicken, pork
Smoked Beers (Rauchbier) ham, bacon, salami, smoked meats
Stout natural oysters, shellfish, crustaceans, desserts (coffee or chocolate-based)
Porter and Oatmeal Stout creamy desserts,
Strong Ales blue cheese, mature cheddar

TASTING NOTES

BEER & BREWERY INDEX

BEER & BREWERY INDEX

ACKNOWLEDGEMENTS

Many heartfelt thanks to Catherine and Maeve, who put up with me, whether I was on the road or hand-cuffed to the keyboard at home. Thanks to the Mountain Goat Brewery for generously accommodating me while I tasted 100-plus imported beers over two days (they helped taste, too!) and for allowing us to photograph bits and pieces around the brewery. Thanks to Blair Hayden and the Lord Nelson pub for their continued support; the Malt Shovel Brewery for providing the beer map on page 187; to Scott Watkins-Sully and other dedicated beer hounds who were my ears, eyes and palate for far-flung breweries I haven't yet visited; and to Fiona Lawrence from Camperdown Cellars who kindly supplied the recommended prices for the 80 imported beers. And for beer lovers everywhere – you make it all worthwhile.